KICK OFF
PREMIERSHIP
2004-05

KICK OFF
PREMIERSHIP
2004-05

Publisher:
Simon Rosen

Editors:
Johanne Springett
Mark Peters

Designers:
Nick Thornton
Ian Bull
Daniel Anim-Kwapong

Statistics Programmers:
Karim Biria
Sean Cronin

Address:
Sidan Press Ltd
22 Seymour Mews
London
W1H 6BZ

Telephone:
020 7486 7117

Email:
Info@sidanpress.com

SIDAN PRESS
Passionate about football

Contents

Season	Champions	Runners-up	Relegated	Promoted
2003-2004	Arsenal	Chelsea	Leeds United Leicester City Wolves	Norwich City WBA Crystal Palace
2002-2003	Manchester Utd	Arsenal	Sunderland West Ham United WBA	Leicester City Portsmouth Wolves
2001-2002	Arsenal	Liverpool	Ipswich Town Derby County Leicester City	Manchester City WBA Birmingham City
2000-2001	Manchester Utd	Arsenal	Manchester City Coventry City Bradford City	Fulham Blackburn Rovers Bolton Wanderers
1999-2000	Manchester Utd	Arsenal	Wimbledon Sheffield Wednesday Watford	Charlton Athletic Manchester City Ipswich Town
1998-1999	Manchester Utd	Arsenal	Charlton Athletic Blackburn Rovers Nottingham Forest	Sunderland Bradford City Watford
1997-1998	Arsenal	Manchester Utd	Bolton Wanderers Barnsley Crystal Palace	Nottingham Forest Middlesbrough Charlton Athletic
1996-1997	Manchester Utd	Newcastle United	Sunderland Middlesbrough Nottingham Forest	Bolton Wanderers Barnsley Crystal Palace
1995-1996	Manchester Utd	Newcastle United	Manchester City QPR Bolton Wanderers	Sunderland Derby County Leicester City
1994-1995	Blackburn Rovers	Manchester Utd	Crystal Palace Norwich City Leicester City Ipswich Town	Middlesbrough Bolton Wanderers
1993-1994	Manchester Utd	Blackburn Rovers	Sheffield United Oldham Athletic Swindon Town	Crystal Palace Nottingham Forest Leicester City
1992-1993	Manchester Utd	Aston Villa	Crystal Palace Middlesbrough Nottingham Forest	Newcastle United West Ham United Swindon Town

Season Statistics 2003-04

Final 2003-04 English Premiership Table

Pos		PL	Home					Away					PTS	GD	
			W	D	L	GF	GA	W	D	L	GF	GA			
1	Arsenal	38	15	4	0	40	14	11	8	0	33	12	90	+47	Champions Lge
2	Chelsea	38	12	4	3	34	13	12	3	4	33	17	79	+37	Champions Lge
3	Man Utd	38	12	4	3	37	15	11	2	6	27	20	75	+29	Champions Lge
4	Liverpool	38	10	4	5	29	15	6	8	5	26	22	60	+18	Champions Lge
5	Newcastle	38	11	5	3	33	14	2	12	5	19	26	56	+12	UEFA Cup
6	Aston Villa	38	9	6	4	24	19	6	5	8	24	25	56	+4	
7	Charlton	38	7	6	6	29	29	7	5	7	22	22	53	0	
8	Bolton	38	6	8	5	24	21	8	3	8	24	35	53	-8	
9	Fulham	38	9	4	6	29	21	5	6	8	23	25	52	+6	
10	Birmingham	38	8	5	6	26	24	4	9	6	17	24	50	-5	
11	Middlesbro	38	8	4	7	25	23	5	5	9	19	29	48	-8	UEFA Cup
12	Southampton	38	8	6	5	24	17	4	5	10	20	28	47	-1	
13	Portsmouth	38	10	4	5	35	19	2	5	12	12	35	45	-7	
14	Tottenham	38	9	4	6	33	27	4	2	13	14	30	45	-10	
15	Blackburn	38	5	4	10	25	31	7	4	8	26	28	44	-8	
16	Man City	38	5	9	5	31	24	4	5	10	24	30	41	+1	
17	Everton	38	8	5	6	27	20	1	7	11	18	37	39	-12	
18	Leicester City	38	3	10	6	19	28	3	5	11	29	37	33	-17	Relegated
19	Leeds Utd	38	5	7	7	25	31	3	2	14	15	48	33	-39	Relegated
20	Wolves	38	7	5	7	23	35	0	7	12	15	42	33	-39	Relegated

Top Goalscorer

Player	Total Goals
T.Henry (Arsenal)	30
A.Shearer (Newcastle United)	22
R.van Nistelrooy (Manchester United)	20
L.Saha (Manchester United)	20
M.Forssell (Birmingham City)	17
Yakubu (Portsmouth)	16
J.Angel (Aston Villa)	16
M.Owen (Liverpool)	16
N.Anelka (Manchester City)	16
J.Beattie (Southampton)	14
R.Keane (Tottenham Hotspur)	14
R.Pires (Arsenal)	14
L.Ferdinand (Leicester City)	12
K.Phillips (Southampton)	12
J.Hasselbaink (Chelsea)	12

Most Goal Assists

Player	Total Assists
S.Malbranque (Fulham)	16
P.Di Canio (Charlton Athletic)	15
M.Izzet (Leicester City)	14
T.Henry (Arsenal)	14
B.Emerton (Blackburn Rovers)	12
R.Giggs (Manchester United)	12
Yabuku (Portsmouth)	11
G.Barry (Aston Villa)	11
K.Davies (Bolton Wanderers)	11
J.Beattie (Southampton)	10
D.Bergkamp (Arsenal)	10
J.Hasselbaink (Chelsea)	10
L.Robert (Newcastle United)	10
R.Pires (Arsenal)	10

Longest Unbeaten Run:

38 matches, Arsenal, 16/08/03 to 15/05/04

Longest Run Without Winning:

14 matches, Man City, 09/11/03 to 11/02/04

Best Home Record: Arsenal, W 15, D 4, L 0, Pts 49

Best Away Record: Arsenal, W 11, D 8, L 0, Pts 41

Highest % of Half-Time Deficits turned into Wins:

Arsenal, 80% (4 out of 5)

Average Goals per Game: 2.66

Most Goals Scored: 73, Arsenal

Most Shots on Target: 233, Liverpool

Highest % of Shot Efficiency:

Chelsea, 67 goals from 203 shots on target (33%)

Longest Scoring Run:

17 matches, Arsenal, 06/12/03 to 09/04/04

Most Goals Scored (Defence): 13, Blackburn

Most Goals Scored (Midfield): 27, Arsenal

Most Goals Scored (Attack): 40, Arsenal

Most Goals (0-15 minutes): 14, Arsenal

Most Goals (16-30 minutes): 12, Chelsea

Most Goals (31-45 minutes): 14, Arsenal

Most Goals (46-60 minutes): 17, Arsenal

Most Goals (61-75 minutes): 15, Fulham

Most Goals (76-90 minutes): 18, Chelsea

Time Period in which Most Goals Scored:

76-90 minutes, 235 out of 1,012 (23%)

Time Period in which Least Goals Scored:

0-15 minutes, 140 out of 1,012 (14%)

Most Goals Scored/Conceded from Open Play:

55 out of 67, Chelsea /57 out of 77 Wolves

Most Goals Scored/Conceded from Corners:

12 out of 51, Charlton /11 out of 57, Tottenham

Most Goals Scored/Conceded from Indirect

Free Kicks: 9 out of 43, Birmingham City & 9 out of 48, Leicester City /12 out of 79, Leeds Utd

Most Goals Scored/Conceded from Direct

Free Kicks: 4 out of 55, Man City & 4 out of 47, Portsmouth /5 out of 59, Blackburn

Most Goals Scored/Conceded from Penalties:

8 out of 55, Liverpool & 8 out of 52, Newcastle Utd 7 out of 57, Everton & 7 out of 79, Leeds Utd

Bookings

Total Yellow Cards: 1070

Average Yellow Cards per Game: 2.82

Total Yellow Cards for Fouls: 822

Total Yellow Cards for Dissent: 109

Total Yellow Cards for Ung. Conduct: 131

Total Yellow Cards for Handball: 8

Most Yellow Cards: 67, Leeds Utd

Most Yellow Cards (Home): 32, Leeds Utd

Most Yellow Cards (Away): 39, Tottenham

Total Red Cards: 58

Total Straight Red Cards: 32

Total Second Bookable Offences: 26

Most Red Cards: 7, Leicester City

Most Red Cards (Home):

3, Birmingham City, Leeds Utd

Most Red Cards (Away): 5, Leicester City

Referee with the Highest Average of Yellow Cards per Game: 3.95, A.G.Wiley

Most Bookings				
F.A. disciplinary points: Yellow=4 points, Two Bookable Offences=10 points, Red Card=12 points				
Player	Y	SB	R	PTS
P.Ince *(Wolves)*	13	1	0	62
L.Boa Morte *(Fulham)*	9	0	1	48
R.Savage *(Birmingham City)*	12	0	0	48
E.Diouf *(Liverpool)*	9	1	0	46
A.Rae *(Wolves)*	9	1	0	46
P.Vieira *(Arsenal)*	9	1	0	46
S.Carr *(Tottenham)*	8	1	0	42
D.Matteo *(Leeds United)*	8	1	0	42
L.Hendrie *(Aston Villa)*	10	0	0	40
D.Mills *(Middlesbrough)*	10	0	0	40
W.Rooney *(Everton)*	10	0	0	40
S.Legwinski *(Fulham)*	7	1	0	38
L.Neill *(Blackburn)*	6	0	1	36
I.Campo *(Bolton)*	9	0	0	36
K.Davies *(Bolton)*	9	0	0	36
G.Flitcroft *(Blackburn)*	9	0	0	36
M.Taricco *(Tottenham)*	9	0	0	36

Arsenal
Manager: **Arsene Wenger**

Club Honours and Records
Premier League: 1997-98, 2001-02, 2003-04
Football League: 1930-31, 1932-33, 1933-34, 1934-35, 1937-38, 1947-48, 1952-53, 1970-71, 1988-89, 1990-91
FA Cup: 1930, 1936, 1950, 1971, 1979, 1993, 1998, 2002, 2003
League Cup: 1987, 1993
Fairs Cup: 1969-70
Cup Winners' Cup: 1993-94

Five Season Form

Games Won	Games Drawn	Games Lost	Goals For	Goals Against	Goal Difference
61%	25%	14%	373	185	+188

Ten Season Form

Prem

12 4 3 1 2 2 2 1 2 1

94-95 95-96 96-97 97-98 98-99 99-00 00-01 01-02 02-03 03-04

Squad List (stats from 2003-04 season)

Position		Appearances	Apps as Sub	Goals/Clean Sheets	Assists	Yellow Cards	Red Cards
G	J.Lehmann	38		15		2	
D	S.Campbell	35		1	1	2	1
D	G.Clichy	7	5			1	
D	A.Cole	32			4	5	1
D	P.Cygan	10	8			1	
D	J.Hoyte		1				
D	M.Keown	3	7			1	
D	Lauren	30	2		1	5	
D	K.Toure	36	1	1	1	4	
M	Edu	13	17	2	3	3	
M	Gilberto	29	3	4	4	2	
M	F.Ljungberg	27	3	4	7	2	
M	R.Parlour	16	9		1	8	
M	R.Pires	33	3	14	10		
M	P.Vieira	29		3	7	9	1
F	J.Aliadiere	3	7			1	
F	D.Bentley	1					
F	D.Bergkamp	21	7	4	10	2	
F	T.Henry	37		30	14	3	
F	N.Kanu	3	7	1	3		
F	J.Reyes	7	6	2	1		
F	S.Wiltord	8	4	3			

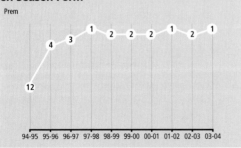

J.Lehmann

S.Campbell
P.Cygan

A.Cole
G.Clichy

K.Toure
M.Keown

Lauren
K.Toure

R.Pires
F.Ljungberg
G.Clichy

P.Vieira
Edu
R.Parlour

Gilberto
Edu
R.Parlour

F.Ljungberg
R.Parlour
S.Wiltord

T.Henry
J.Aliadiere

D.Bergkamp
J.Reyes
S.Wiltord

Top Goalscorer
Thierry Henry

30 Goals

Left Foot	Right Foot	Header
6	23	1

Total

% of team's goals **41%**

Goal Breakdown
(stats from 2003-04 season)

	Set Piece	Open Play	Total
Thierry Henry	11	19	30
Robert Pires	-	14	14
Dennis Bergkamp	-	4	4
Fredrik Ljungberg		4	4
Gilberto	2	2	4
Patrick Vieira	-	3	3
Sylvain Wiltord		3	3
Edu	2	-	2
Jose Antonio Reyes	-	2	2
Sol Campbell	1	-	1
Nwankwo Kanu	-	1	1
Kolo Toure	1	-	1

Premiership Statistics

First Goal Scored (average)

Home	Away
27	**26**
mins	mins

First Goal Conceded (average)

Home	Away
28	**25**
mins	mins

Clean Sheets	Failed To Score
15	**4**
	matches

Corners per game (average)	Average shots on target
5	**6**

Most Common Result:
2-1 (ten times)

Most First Goals:
15 – Thierry Henry

Hat-Tricks:
4 - Thierry Henry v Leeds (H)
3 - Thierry Henry v Liverpool (H)

Fastest Goal (mins):
2 - Robert Pires v Charlton (H)

Fastest Booking (mins):
7 - Ray Parlour v Chelsea (H)

Highest Attendance:
38,419 v Leicester City 15/05/04

Lowest Attendance:
37,677 v Blackburn 14/12/03

Average Attendance: 38,078

1   1   1   2   2   1   1   1   1   1

Season Progression

Pos		W	D	L	Pts
1	Arsenal	26	12	0	90

AUG   SEPT   OCT   NOV   DEC   JAN   FEB   MAR   APR   MAY

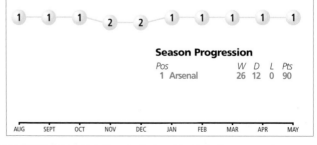

Arsenal

Enhanced Fixture List 2004-05

In this fixture...

	Date	Opposition	03-04 scoreline	Played	Premiership history	Goals for	Goals against	No. of times Arsenal scored first and the result that followed ⚽ ►		W	D	L	Most common score (no. times)	Avg time of first goal (mins)	Avg no. of corners
	15th Aug	Everton	1 - 1	12	DDDWWDWWLWLD	14	9	9	►	5	3	1	1-1 (3x)	35	4
	22nd Aug	Middlesbro	4 - 1	9	D--DW-DWLWWW	18	9	4	►	4	0	0	1-1 (3x)	48	9
	24th Aug	Blackburn	1 - 0	10	LWDDDLW--DLW	9	10	5	►	3	1	1	1-0 (3x)	36	8
	28th Aug	Norwich	n/a	3	DDD---------	2	2	1	►	0	1	0	1-1 (2x)	57	8
	11th Sep	Fulham	1 - 0	3	---------WWW	5	1	3	►	3	0	0	0-1 (2x)	19	5
	18th Sep	Bolton	2 - 1	5	---W-W---DWW	11	5	3	►	2	1	0	2-1 (3x)	44	9
	25th Sep	Man City	2 - 1	7	WDWW----W-WW	15	3	5	►	5	0	0	1-2 (2x)	43	5
	2nd Oct	Charlton	2 - 1	5	------D-WLWW	11	8	4	►	3	0	1	5-3 (1x)	13	8
	16th Oct	Aston Villa	2 - 0	12	LLDWDDWWWWWW	18	9	7	►	5	1	1	3-1 (2x)	46	8
	24th Oct	Man Utd	0 - 0	12	DLLLLWDDLWLD	5	16	4	►	2	2	0	1-0 (3x)	42	4
	30th Oct	Southampton	2 - 0	12	WWDWWWDWWDWW	30	11	11	►	8	3	0	1-1 (3x)	35	9
	6th Nov	C Palace	n/a	3	W-W--D------	5	1	2	►	2	0	0	1-2 (1x)	15	5
	13th Nov	Tottenham	2 - 2	12	LWLLDDWLDDDD	12	13	5	►	2	2	1	1-1 (4x)	48	5
	20th Nov	West Brom	n/a	1	----------W-	5	2	1	►	1	0	0	5-2 (1x)	3	1
	28th Nov	Liverpool	2 - 1	12	WDLLLLDLLWDW	9	22	4	►	2	1	1	4-0 (2x)	29	5
	4th Dec	Birmingham	0 - 0	2	----------WD	2	0	1	►	1	0	0	2-0 (1x)	9	6
	12th Dec	Chelsea	2 - 1	12	WWWDDWWWDWWW	23	12	8	►	7	1	0	2-1 (4x)	31	6
	19th Dec	Portsmouth	1 - 1	1	-----------D	1	1	0	►	0	0	0	1-1 (1x)	50	12
	26th Dec	Fulham	0 - 0	3	---------WWD	6	2	2	►	2	0	0	4-1 (1x)	11	7

Home fixture (shirt icon)

Date	Opposition	03-04 scoreline	Played	Premiership history	Goals for	Goals against	No. of times Arsenal scored first	►	W	D	L	Most common score (no. times)	Avg time of first goal (mins)	Avg no. of corners	Home fixture
29th Dec	Newcastle	0 - 0	11	-LLLWWDLDWDD	9	12	5	►	3	2	0	2-0 (2x)	23	5	
1st Jan	Charlton	1 - 1	5	------W-LWWD	8	2	3	►	3	0	0	0-3 (2x)	38	7	
3rd Jan	Man City	2 - 1	7	WDWW----W-WW	16	3	6	►	6	0	0	2-1 (2x)	27	7	(shirt)
15th Jan	Bolton	1 - 1	5	---L-W---WDD	6	4	4	►	2	2	0	2-2 (1x)	47	5	
22nd Jan	Newcastle	3 - 2	11	-WLWLWWDWLWW	22	11	8	►	7	0	1	5-0 (1x)	18	7	(shirt)
1st Feb	Man Utd	1 - 1	12	LDDWLWWLWWDD	18	13	6	►	4	1	1	2-2 (2x)	36	6	(shirt)
5th Feb	Aston Villa	2 - 0	12	LWWDDLLDDWDW	17	12	7	►	4	2	1	1-1 (3x)	43	4	
12th Feb	C Palace	n/a	3	W-L--W------	5	2	2	►	2	0	0	3-0 (1x)	43	7	(shirt)
26th Feb	Southampton	1 - 0	12	LWLDWWDWLWLW	17	10	8	►	6	0	2	3-2 (2x)	32	5	
5th Mar	Portsmouth	1 - 1	1	-----------D	1	1	0	►	0	0	0	1-1 (1x)	40	8	(shirt)
19th Mar	Blackburn	2 - 0	10	LDLDWWW--WLW	16	12	5	►	5	0	0	1-1 (2x)	37	5	
2nd Apr	Norwich	n/a	3	LDW---------	7	5	2	►	1	0	1	5-1 (1x)	16	7	(shirt)
7th Apr	Liverpool	4 - 2	12	LWLDLLDLWDDW	10	10	3	►	2	1	0	0-1 (4x)	51	7	(shirt)
9th Apr	Middlesbro	4 - 0	9	L--WW-WLWWWW	23	6	7	►	7	0	0	0-4 (2x)	25	6	
16th Apr	Everton	2 - 1	12	WWDLWWWWWWWW	30	11	11	►	9	1	1	4-1 (2x)	22	8	(shirt)
20th Apr	Chelsea	2 - 1	12	LWLLWWDWDDDW	18	13	3	►	2	1	0	2-3 (2x)	40	4	
23rd Apr	Tottenham	2 - 1	12	LDDDWDDWWWWW	17	9	6	►	5	1	0	2-1 (3x)	45	8	(shirt)
30th Apr	West Brom	n/a	1	----------W-	2	1	0	►	0	0	0	1-2 (1x)	48	5	
14th May	Birmingham	3 - 0	2	----------WW	7	0	2	►	2	0	0	0-4 (1x)	5	6	

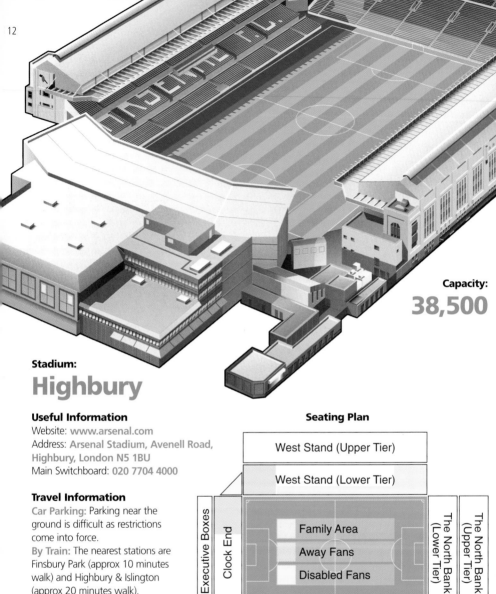

Capacity:

38,500

Stadium:

Highbury

Useful Information

Website: www.arsenal.com
Address: Arsenal Stadium, Avenell Road,
Highbury, London N5 1BU
Main Switchboard: 020 7704 4000

Travel Information

Car Parking: Parking near the
ground is difficult as restrictions
come into force.
By Train: The nearest stations are
Finsbury Park (approx 10 minutes
walk) and Highbury & Islington
(approx 20 minutes walk).
By Tube: Arsenal is the nearest
tube station.
By Bus: Numbers 19, 106, 153 and 236
go to Blackstock Road, the ground is
approximately a 10 minute walk.

Seating Plan

| West Stand (Upper Tier) |
| West Stand (Lower Tier) |

Executive Boxes | Clock End | Family Area / Away Fans / Disabled Fans | The North Bank (Lower Tier) | The North Bank (Upper Tier)

| East Stand (Lower Tier) |
| East Stand (Upper Tier) |

Area Map

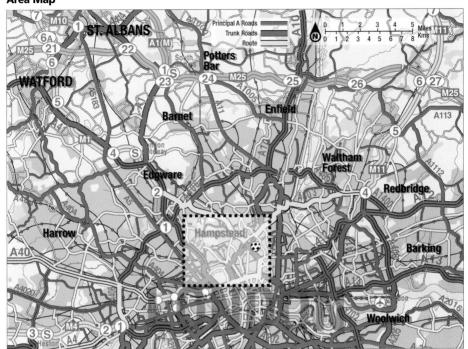

Local Map

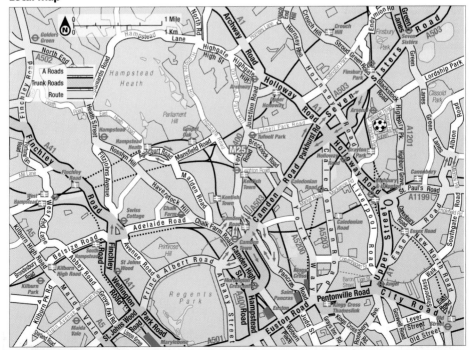

Aston Villa

Manager: **David O'Leary**

Club Honours and Records

Football League: 1893-94, 1895-96, 1896-97, 1898-1899, 1899-1900, 1909-1910, 1980-81
Division 2: 1937-38, 1959-60
Division 3: 1971-72
FA Cup: 1887, 1895, 1897, 1905, 1913, 1920, 1957
League Cup: 1961, 1975, 1977, 1994, 1996
European Cup: 1981-82
European Super Cup: 1982-83

Five Season Form

Games Won	Games Drawn	Games Lost	Goals For	Goals Against	Goal Difference
35%	33%	32%	197	216	-19

Ten Season Form

Prem

94-95 95-96 96-97 97-98 98-99 99-00 00-01 01-02 02-03 03-04

Squad List (stats from 2003-04 season)	Position	Appearances	Apps as Sub	Goals/Clean Sheets	Assists	Yellow Cards	Red Cards
G	S.Postma		2				
G	T.Sorensen	38		12		1	
D	O.Alpay	4	2	1			
D	U.De la Cruz	20	8		1	2	
D	M.Delaney	23	2		3	4	
D	R.Johnsen	21	2	1		3	
D	O.Mellberg	33		1	1	4	
D	L.Ridgewell	5	6		1		
D	J.Samuel	38		2	4	6	
M	G.Barry	36		3	11	3	1
M	M.Hadji		1				
M	L.Hendrie	32		2	4	10	
M	T.Hitzlsperger	22	10	3	8	4	
M	M.Kinsella	2					
M	G.McCann	28				4	1
M	N.Solano	10			2	1	1
M	P.Whittingham	20	12		3	4	
F	M.Allback	7	8	1			
F	J.Angel	33		16	1	3	
F	P.Crouch	6	10	4	2	1	
F	D.Dublin	12	11	3		1	
F	L.Moore		7			1	
F	S.Moore	2	6	1			
F	D.Vassell	26	6	9	2		

T.Sorensen
S.Postma

J.Samuel

R.Johnsen
D.Dublin
L.Ridgewell

O.Mellberg
D.Dublin

G.Barry
P.Whittingham

U.De la Cruz
M.Delaney

T.Hitzlsperger
G.Barry
P.Whittingham

G.McCann
L.Hendrie

L.Hendrie
N.Solano
U.De la Cruz

J.Angel
P.Crouch

D.Vassell
M.Allback

Top Goalscorer
Juan Pablo Angel

16 Goals

	Left Foot	Right Foot	Header
Total	0	11	5

% of team's goals **33%**

Goal Breakdown
(stats from 2003-04 season)

	Set Piece	Open Play	Total
Juan Pablo Angel	5	11	**16**
Darius Vassell	3	6	**9**
Peter Crouch	1	3	**4**
Dion Dublin	3	-	**3**
Gareth Barry	2	1	**3**
Thomas Hitzlsperger	-	3	**3**
Lee Hendrie	-	2	**2**
Jlloyd Samuel	-	2	**2**
Ronny Johnsen	1	-	**1**
Alpay	1	-	**1**
Stefan Moore	1	-	**1**
Olof Mellberg	1	-	**1**
Marcus Allback	-	1	**1**

Premiership Statistics

First Goal Scored (average)

Home	Away
19 mins	**24** mins

First Goal Conceded (average)

Home	Away
27 mins	**31** mins

Clean Sheets	Failed To Score
12	**14** matches

Corners Per Game (average)	Average shots on target
7	**5**

Most Common Result:
0-2 (six times)

Most First Goals:
11 - Juan Pablo Angel

Hat-Tricks:
None

Fastest Goal (mins):
5 – Juan Pablo Angel v Tottenham (H).

Fastest Booking (mins):
9 – Olof Mellberg v Leicester (A).

Highest Attendance:
42,573 v Liverpool 24/08/03.

Lowest Attendance:
28,625 v Portsmouth 06/01/04.

Average Attendance: 36,621

Season Progression

12 11 14 17 10 11 7 7 5 6

Pos
6 Aston Villa

W	D	L	Pts
15	11	12	56

AUG SEPT OCT NOV DEC JAN FEB MAR APR MAY

Aston Villa

Enhanced Fixture List 2004-05

In this fixture...

	Date	Opposition	03-04 scoreline	Played	Premiership history	Goals for	Goals against	No. of times Aston Villa scored first and the result that followed					Most common score (no. times)	Avg time of first goal (mins)	Avg no. of corners
								⚽	►	W	D	L			
👕	14th Aug	Southampton	1 - 0	12	DLDWWDWLDWLW	13	8	8	►	5	3	0	1-1 (3x)	38	5
	22nd Aug	West Brom	n/a	1	----------D-	0	0	0	►	0	0	0	0-0 (1x)	N/A	6
	24th Aug	Charlton	2 - 1	5	------W-DWLW	8	8	2	►	2	0	0	1-2 (2x)	24	6
👕	28th Aug	Newcastle	0 - 0	11	-LLDDLWLDDLD	6	12	3	►	1	2	0	1-1 (3x)	31	7
👕	11th Sep	Chelsea	3 - 2	12	LWWLLLLDDDWW	12	16	6	►	3	2	1	1-1 (2x)	19	6
	18th Sep	Norwich	n/a	3	LWD---------	3	3	1	►	0	1	0	1-2 (1x)	31	2
👕	25th Sep	Crystal	n/a	3	W-D--W------	7	2	3	►	2	1	0	3-1 (1x)	22	4
	2nd Oct	Blackburn	2 - 0	10	LLLDWLL--LDW	7	18	3	►	2	1	0	3-0 (2x)	66	3
	16th Oct	Arsenal	0 - 2	12	WWDLDDLLLLLL	9	18	3	►	1	0	2	3-1 (2x)	57	5
👕	23rd Oct	Fulham	3 - 0	3	---------WWW	8	1	3	►	3	0	0	3-1 (1x)	34	6
	30th Oct	Everton	0 - 2	12	LWDLWWDDWLLL	12	12	5	►	4	0	1	0-1 (3x)	54	5
👕	6th Nov	Portsmouth	2 - 1	1	-----------W	2	1	1	►	1	0	0	2-1 (1x)	22	9
	13th Nov	Bolton	2 - 2	5	---W-W---LLD	7	6	3	►	2	1	0	3-2 (1x)	21	4
👕	22nd Nov	Tottenham	1 - 0	12	DWWWDWWDWDLW	17	8	7	►	7	0	0	1-1 (3x)	45	8
	27th Nov	Man City	1 - 4	7	DLDL----W-LL	8	15	2	►	0	1	1	4-1 (1x)	35	5
👕	4th Dec	Liverpool	0 - 0	12	WWWLWWWLDLLLD	14	16	2	►	2	0	0	2-1 (2x)	42	7
👕	12th Dec	Birmingham	2 - 2	2	----------LD	2	4	1	►	0	1	0	2-2 (1x)	21	6
	18th Dec	Middlesbro	2 - 1	9	W--WL-DWDLWW	20	11	5	►	4	1	0	3-2 (1x)	39	4
	26th Dec	Chelsea	0 - 1	12	WDLWDWLLLWLL	10	12	5	►	3	2	0	1-0 (4x)	32	4

Date	Opposition	03-04 scoreline	Played	Premiership history	Goals for	Goals against	⚽	►	W	D	L	Most common score (no. times)	Avg time of first goal (mins)	Avg no. of corners	
28th Dec	Man Utd	0 - 2	12	WLLWDLDLLDLL	8	14	4	►	2	1	1	0-1 (3x)	27	5	👕
1st Jan	Blackburn	0 - 2	10	DLLWWLL--WWL	9	11	4	►	4	0	0	2-0 (2x)	47	6	👕
3rd Jan	C Palace	n/a	3	L-D--D------	1	2	0	►	0	0	0	1-1 (1x)	86	7	
15th Jan	Norwich	n/a	3	LDD---------	3	4	0	►	0	0	0	2-3 (1x)	54	10	👕
22nd Jan	Man Utd	0 - 4	12	DLLDDLLLLLDL	4	19	2	►	0	2	0	1-0 (3x)	53	5	
2nd Feb	Fulham	2 - 1	3	---------DLW	3	3	1	►	0	0	1	2-1 (1x)	8	5	
5th Feb	Arsenal	0 - 2	12	WLLDDWWDDLDL	12	17	4	►	2	2	0	1-1 (3x)	56	5	
12th Feb	Portsmouth	1 - 2	1	-----------L	1	2	0	►	0	0	0	2-1 (1x)	84	9	
26th Feb	Everton	0 - 0	12	WDDWWWWWWDWD	19	6	6	►	6	0	0	0-0 (4x)	28	6	👕
5th Mar	Middlesbro	0 - 2	9	W--DW-WWDDWL	12	5	6	►	5	1	0	1-0 (3x)	21	5	👕
19th Mar	Birmingham	0 - 0	2	----------LD	0	3	0	►	0	0	0	3-0 (1x)	N/A	5	
2nd Apr	Newcastle	1 - 1	11	-LLLLLLWLLDD	9	24	4	►	1	1	2	3-0 (2x)	39	4	
7th Apr	Man City	1 - 1	7	WDDL----D-WD	8	6	3	►	1	2	0	1-1 (2x)	43	5	👕
9th Apr	West Brom	n/a	1	----------W-	2	1	1	►	1	0	0	2-1 (1x)	16	7	👕
16th Apr	Southampton	1 - 1	12	LLLWWWWLLWDD	16	18	7	►	5	2	0	2-0 (3x)	32	4	
20th Apr	Charlton	2 - 1	5	------L-WWWW	10	6	4	►	4	0	0	2-1 (1x)	31	7	👕
23rd Apr	Bolton	1 - 1	5	---W-L---WWD	8	6	2	►	2	0	0	3-2 (1x)	42	8	👕
30th Apr	Tottenham	1 - 2	12	DDWWLLLWDDLL	13	14	4	►	2	1	1	1-0 (3x)	40	6	
14th May	Liverpool	0 - 1	12	WLLLLLWDLWDL	11	21	2	►	2	0	0	3-0 (3x)	49	5	

Stadium:

Villa Park

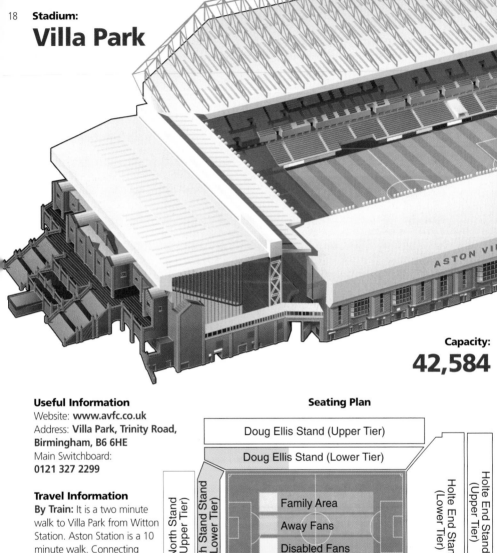

Capacity:

42,584

Useful Information

Website: **www.avfc.co.uk**
Address: **Villa Park, Trinity Road,
Birmingham, B6 6HE**
Main Switchboard:
0121 327 2299

Travel Information

By Train: It is a two minute
walk to Villa Park from Witton
Station. Aston Station is a 10
minute walk. Connecting
trains run from Birmingham
New Street.
By Bus: The number 7 runs
from Birmingham City Centre
directly to the ground. Numbers
11a and 11c also serve the ground.

Seating Plan

Doug Ellis Stand (Upper Tier)

Doug Ellis Stand (Lower Tier)

North Stand (Upper Tier)

North Stand Stand (Lower Tier)

Family Area

Away Fans

Disabled Fans

Holte End Stand (Lower Tier)

Holte End Stand (Upper Tier)

Trinity Road Stand (Lower Tier)

Trinity Road Stand (Upper Tier)

Area Map

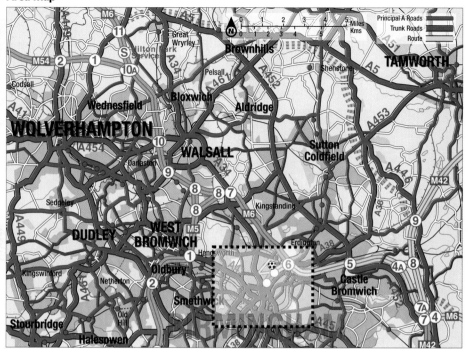

Local Map

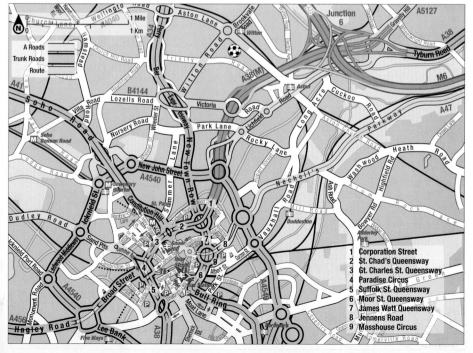

1 Corporation Street
2 St. Chad's Queensway
3 Gt. Charles St. Queensway
4 Paradise Circus
5 Suffolk St. Queensway
6 Moor St. Queensway
7 James Watt Queensway
8 Jennens Road
9 Masshouse Circus

Birmingham City
Manager: **Steve Bruce**

Club Honours and Records
Division 2: 1892-93, 1920-21, 1947-48, 1954-55, 1994-95
League Cup: 1963

Squad List (stats from 2003-04 season)

Position		Appearances	Apps as Sub	Goals/Clean Sheets	Assists	Yellow Cards	Red Cards
G	I.Bennett	4	2	2			
G	Maik Taylor	34		13			2
D	J.Clapham	22	3		1		
D	K.Cunningham	36			2	2	1
D	M.Grainger	3	1	1	1		
D	J.Kenna	14	3	2		1	
D	D.Purse	9					1
D	Martin Taylor	11	1	1			
D	O.Tebily	17	10			4	
D	M.Upson	30			2	2	
M	D.Carter	1	4				
M	A.Cisse	5	10			5	
M	S.Clemence	32	3	2	2	4	
M	P.Devlin		2				
M	D.Dunn	20	1	2	2	2	
M	B.Hughes	17	9	3	1		
M	D.Johnson	35		1	6	6	
M	J.Kirovski		6				
M	S.Lazaridis	25	5	2	5		
M	R.Savage	31		3	6	12	
F	A.Barrowman		1				
F	C.Dugarry	12	2	1	1	4	1
F	L.Figueroa		1				
F	M.Forssell	32		17	4	1	
F	G.Horsfield	2	1				
F	S.John	7	22	4			
F	C.Morrison	19	13	4		6	1

Five Season Form

Games Won	Games Drawn	Games Lost	Goals For	Goals Against	Goal Difference
43%	26%	31%	219	238	-19

Ten Season Form

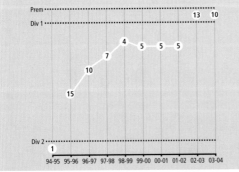

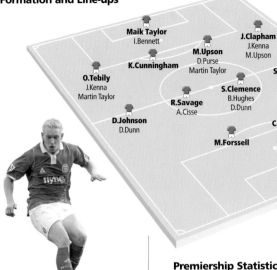

Maik Taylor
I.Bennett

J.Clapham
J.Kenna
M.Upson

M.Upson
D.Purse
Martin Taylor

K.Cunningham

S.Lazaridis
D.Dunn
B.Hughes

O.Tebily
J.Kenna
Martin Taylor

S.Clemence
B.Hughes
D.Dunn

R.Savage
A.Cisse

D.Johnson
D.Dunn

C.Morrison
S.John
C.Dugarry

M.Forssell

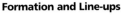

Top Goalscorer
Mikael Forssell

17 Goals

	Left Foot	Right Foot	Header
Total	7	8	2

% of team's goals **40%**

Goal Breakdown
(stats from 2003-04 season)

	Set Piece	Open Play	Total
Mikael Forssell	7	10	17
Clinton Morrison	1	3	4
Stern John	1	3	4
Robbie Savage	3	-	3
Bryan Hughes	-	3	3
Jeff Kenna	1	1	2
Stan Lazaridis	-	2	2
Stephen Clemence	2	-	2
David Dunn	2	-	2
Damien Johnson	1	-	1
Martin Taylor	1	-	1
Martin Grainger	1	-	1
Christophe Dugarry	1	-	1

Premiership Statistics
First Goal Scored (average)

Home	Away
26 mins	**36** mins

First Goal Conceded (average)

Home	Away
19 mins	**21** mins

Clean Sheets	Failed To Score
15	**13** matches

Corners Per Game (average)	Average shots on target
5	**4**

Season Progression

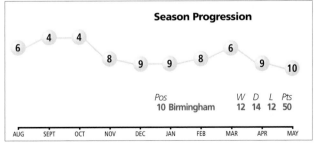

6   4   4   8   9   9   8   6   9   10

Pos		W	D	L	Pts
10 Birmingham		12	14	12	50

AUG   SEPT   OCT   NOV   DEC   JAN   FEB   MAR   APR   MAY

Most Common Result:
0-0 (seven times)

Most First Goals:
8 - Mikael Forssell

Hat-Tricks:
None

Fastest Goal (mins):
8 – Damien Johnson v Everton (H)

Fastest Booking (mins):
3 - Christophe Dugarry v Charlton Athletic (H).

Highest Attendance:
29,588 v Arsenal 22/11/03.

Lowest Attendance:
27,225 v Charlton 03/11/03.

Average Attendance: 29,077

Birmingham City

Enhanced Fixture List 2004-05

In this fixture...

Date	Opposition	03-04 scoreline	Played	Premiership history	Goals for	Goals against	⚽	►	W	D	L	Most common score (no. times)	Avg time of first goal (mins)	Avg no. corners
14th Aug	Portsmouth	1 - 3	1	----------L	1	3	0	►	0	0	0	3-1 (1x)	67	4
21st Aug	Chelsea	0 - 0	2	----------LD	1	3	0	►	0	0	0	1-3 (1x)	87	5
24th Aug	Man City	2 - 1	2	----------LW	2	3	0	►	0	0	0	2-1 (1x)	81	8
28th Aug	Tottenham	1 - 4	2	----------LL	2	6	0	►	0	0	0	4-1 (1x)	73	5
11th Sep	Middlesbro	3 - 5	2	----------LL	3	6	0	►	0	0	0	5-3 (1x)	23	5
18th Sep	Charlton	1 - 2	2	----------DL	2	3	0	►	0	0	0	1-2 (1x)	66	9
25th Sep	Bolton	1 - 0	2	----------LW	3	4	1	►	1	0	0	4-2 (1x)	38	11
2nd Oct	Newcastle	1 - 1	2	----------LD	1	3	0	►	0	0	0	1-1 (1x)	90	4
16th Oct	Man Utd	1 - 2	2	----------LL	1	3	1	►	0	0	1	1-2 (1x)	39	2
24th Oct	Southampton	0 - 0	2	----------LD	0	2	0	►	0	0	0	2-0 (1x)	N/A	8
30th Oct	C Palace	n/a		These teams have never played each other in the Premiership										
6th Nov	Liverpool	1 - 3	2	----------DL	3	5	1	►	0	0	1	3-1 (1x)	47	3
13th Nov	Everton	3 - 0	2	----------DW	4	1	1	►	1	0	0	3-0 (1x)	27	4
21st Nov	Blackburn	1 - 1	2	----------DD	2	2	0	►	0	0	0	1-1 (2x)	83	10
27th Nov	Norwich	n/a		These teams have never played each other in the Premiership										
4th Dec	Arsenal	0 - 0	2	----------LD	0	2	0	►	0	0	0	2-0 (1x)	N/A	3
12th Dec	Aston Villa	2 - 2	2	----------WD	4	2	1	►	1	0	0	2-2 (1x)	67	4
18th Dec	West Brom	n/a	1	----------W-	1	0	1	►	1	0	0	1-0 (1x)	90	7
26th Dec	Middlesbro	3 - 1	2	----------WW	6	1	2	►	2	0	0	3-1 (1x)	21	4

Home fixture

Date	Opposition	03-04 scoreline	Played	Premiership history	Goals for	Goals against	⚽	▶	W	D	L	Most common score (no. times)	Avg time of first goal (mins)	Avg no of corners	
28th Dec	Fulham	0 - 0	2	----------WD	1	0	1	▶	1	0	0	0-1 (1x)	7	2	
1st Jan	Newcastle	1 - 0	2	----------LW	1	1	1	▶	1	0	0	1-0 (1x)	61	5	
3rd Jan	Bolton	2 - 0	2	----------WW	5	1	2	▶	2	0	0	3-1 (1x)	43	6	
15th Jan	Charlton	1 - 1	2	----------WD	3	1	2	▶	1	1	0	1-1 (1x)	52	4	
22nd Jan	Fulham	2 - 2	2	----------DD	2	2	0	▶	0	0	0	2-2 (1x)	45	12	
1st Feb	Southampton	2 - 1	2	----------WW	5	3	0	▶	0	0	0	3-2 (1x)	46	6	
5th Feb	Man Utd	0 - 3	2	----------LL	0	5	0	▶	0	0	0	3-0 (1x)	N/A	3	
12th Feb	Liverpool	0 - 3	2	----------WL	2	4	1	▶	1	0	0	2-1 (1x)	34	3	
26th Feb	C Palace	n/a		These teams have never played each other in the Premiership											
5th Mar	West Brom	n/a	1	----------D-	1	1	1	▶	0	1	0	1-1 (1x)	86	2	
19th Mar	Aston Villa	0 - 0	2	----------WD	3	0	1	▶	1	0	0	3-0 (1x)	31	5	
2nd Apr	Tottenham	1 - 0	2	----------DW	2	1	1	▶	1	0	0	1-1 (1x)	52	1	
9th Apr	Chelsea	0 - 0	2	----------LD	0	3	0	▶	0	0	0	3-0 (1x)	N/A	3	
16th Apr	Portsmouth	2 - 0	1	----------W	2	0	1	▶	1	0	0	2-0 (1x)	21	4	
20th Apr	Man City	0 - 0	2	----------LD	0	1	0	▶	0	0	0	1-0 (1x)	N/A	6	
23rd Apr	Everton	0 - 1	2	----------DL	1	2	1	▶	0	1	0	1-1 (1x)	50	3	
30th Apr	Blackburn	0 - 4	2	----------LL	0	5	0	▶	0	0	0	0-4 (1x)	N/A	8	
7th May	Norwich	n/a		These teams have never played each other in the Premiership											
14th May	Arsenal	0 - 3	2	----------LL	0	7	0	▶	0	0	0	0-4 (1x)	N/A	7	

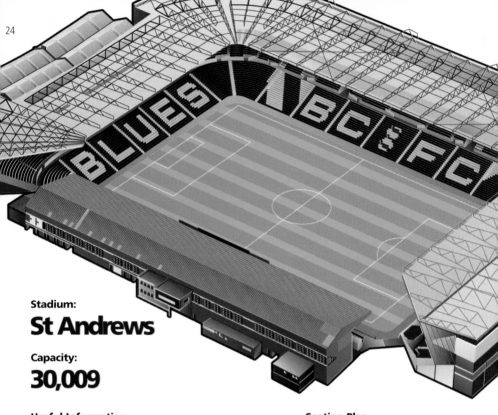

Stadium:

St Andrews

Capacity:

30,009

Useful Information

Website: **www.bcfc.com**
Address: **St Andrews Stadium, Birmingham B9 4NH**
Main Switchboard:
0121 772 0101

Travel Information

By Train: Birmingham New Street and Birmingham Moor Street are both roughly 20 minutes walk from the ground. Taxis from the station to the ground cost around £3.50.
By Bus: Numbers 56, 57, 57a, 58 and 60 run from the city centre to the ground. Numbers 15, 17, 96 and 97 also stop near the stadium.

Seating Plan

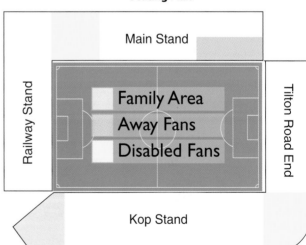

Main Stand

Railway Stand

Family Area

Away Fans

Disabled Fans

Tilton Road End

Kop Stand

Area Map

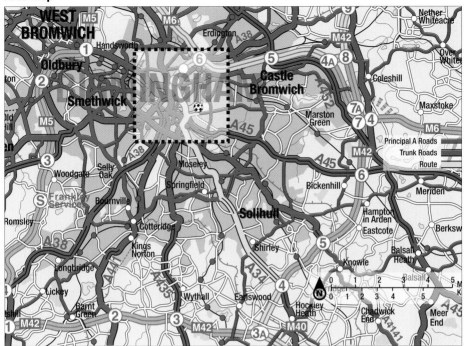

Local Map

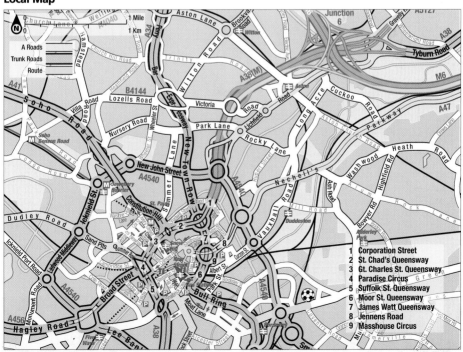

1 Corporation Street
2 St. Chad's Queensway
3 Gt. Charles St. Queensway
4 Paradise Circus
5 Suffolk St. Queensway
6 Moor St. Queensway
7 James Watt Queensway
8 Jennens Road
9 Masshouse Circus

Blackburn Rovers

Manager: **Graeme Souness**

Club Honours and Records
Premier League: 1994-95
Football League: 1911-12, 1913-14
Division 2: 1938-39
Division 3: 1974-75
FA Cup: 1884, 1885, 1886, 1890, 1891, 1928
League Cup: 2002
Full Members Cup: 1987

Five Season Form

Games Won	Games Drawn	Games Lost	Goals For	Goals Against	Goal Difference
39%	**29%**	**32%**	**237**	**243**	**-6**

Ten Season Form

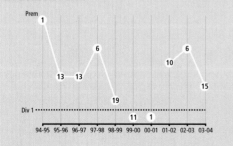

Squad List (stats from 2003-04 season)

Position		Appearances	Apps as Sub	Goals/Clean Sheets	Assists	Yellow Card	Red Card
G	P.Enckelman	2					
G	B.Friedel	36		1/8			
D	L.Amoruso	11	1	3		3	
D	M.Babbel	23	2	3	1	2	
D	M.Gray	14				1	
D	V.Gresko	22	2	1	1	6	
D	N.Johansson	7	7				
D	L.Neill	30	2	2		6	1
D	C.Short	19		1		1	
D	M.Taylor	10	1				
D	A.Todd	19			1	4	
M	M.Andresen	11				3	
M	D.Baggio		9	1		1	
M	N.Danns		1				
M	J.Douglas	14		1		3	
M	B.Emerton	31	6	2	12	4	
M	B.Ferguson	14	1	1	2	3	
M	G.Flitcroft	29	2	3	2	9	
M	A.Mahon	1	2				
M	S.Reid	9	7			1	1
M	D.Thompson	10	1	1	2	5	
M	K.Tugay	30	6	1	8	4	
F	A.Cole	27	7	11	7	3	1
F	P.Gallagher	12	14	3	5	2	
F	C.Grabbi		5		1		
F	M.Jansen	9	10	2	2		
F	J.Stead	13		6			
F	D.Yorke	15	8	4	2		

Formation and Line-ups

B.Friedel
P.Enckelman

V.Gresko
M.Gray

C.Short
A.Todd
N.Johansson

L.Amoruso
M.Babbel
M.Taylor

J.Douglas
D.Thompson

L.Neill
M.Babbel
S.Reid

Tugay
B.Ferguson

G.Flitcroft
M.Andresen
B.Ferguson

B.Emerton
G.Flitcroft

A.Cole
M.Jansen
P.Gallagher

J.Stead
D.Yorke
M.Jansen
P.Gallagher

Top Goalscorer
Andy Cole

11 Goals

	Left Foot	Right Foot	Header
Total	**2**	**9**	**-**

% of team's goals **22%**

Goal Breakdown
(stats from 2003-04 season)

	Set Piece	Open Play	Total
Andy Cole	1	10	**11**
Jonathan Stead	1	5	**6**
Dwight Yorke	1	3	**4**
Garry Flitcroft		3	**3**
Markus Babbel	3		**3**
Lorenzo Amoruso	3		**3**
Paul Gallagher		3	**3**
Matt Jansen		2	**2**
Lucas Neill	1	1	**2**
Brett Emerton		2	**2**
Others	3	5	**8**

Premiership Statistics

First Goal Scored (average)

Home	Away
30 mins	**36** mins

First Goal Conceded (average)

Home	Away
27 mins	**24** mins

Clean Sheets	Failed To Score
8	**9** matches

Corners Per Game (average)	Average shots on target
6	**5**

Most Common Result:
1-0 (six times)

Most First Goals:
6 - Andy Cole

Hat-Tricks:
None

Fastest Goal (mins):
1 - Andy Cole v Chelsea (A).

Fastest Booking (mins):
6 - Vratislav Gresko v Arsenal (A).

Highest Attendance:
30,074 v Liverpool 13/09/03.

Lowest Attendance:
19,939 v Charlton 20/10/03.

Average Attendance: 24,376

Season Progression

6 · 4 · 4 · 8 · 9 · 9 · 8 · 6 · 9 · 10

Pos		W	D	L	Pts
15 Blackburn		12	8	18	44

AUG SEPT OCT NOV DEC JAN FEB MAR APR MAY

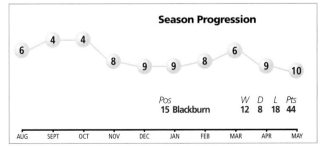

Blackburn Rovers

Enhanced Fixture List 2004-05

In this fixture...

Date	Opposition	03-04 scoreline	Played	Premiership history	Goals for	Goals against	⚽	►	W	D	L	Most common score (no. times)	Avg time of first goal (mins)	Avg no. corn.
14th Aug	West Brom	n/a	1	----------D-	1	1	1	►	0	1	0	1-1 (1x)	11	7
21st Aug	Southampton	0 - 2	10	DLDLLLD--WDL	9	18	1	►	0	1	0	1-1 (3x)	49	6
24th Aug	Arsenal	0 - 1	10	WLDDDWL--DWL	10	9	3	►	2	1	0	1-0 (3x)	53	3
28th Aug	Man Utd	1 - 0	10	DWLLLLD--DWW	12	14	5	►	3	0	2	1-0 (2x)	45	5
11th Sep	Newcastle	1 - 0	9	-DDLLDD--LLW	8	14	4	►	1	2	1	1-1 (4x)	59	5
18th Sep	Portsmouth	1 - 2	1	----------L	1	2	0	►	0	0	0	1-2 (1x)	37	5
27th Sep	Charlton	2 - 3	4	------D--WLL	5	6	1	►	1	0	0	3-2 (1x)	63	8
2nd Oct	Aston Villa	0 - 2	10	WWWDLWW--WDL	18	7	6	►	6	0	0	3-0 (2x)	23	7
16th Oct	Middlesbro	2 - 2	7	D--WD-D--LWD	5	4	4	►	2	2	0	1-0 (2x)	31	6
23rd Oct	Chelsea	2 - 2	10	DWWWDWD--DWD	14	9	5	►	3	2	0	1-2 (3x)	51	4
30th Oct	Liverpool	1 - 3	10	WWWLWDL--DDL	20	16	5	►	3	1	1	1-3 (2x)	33	7
6th Nov	Norwich	n/a	3	DDL---------	3	4	2	►	0	1	1	2-2 (1x)	18	9
13th Nov	Man City	1 - 1	6	LWWD------DD	11	8	5	►	2	2	1	1-1 (2x)	27	4
21st Nov	Birmingham	1 - 1	2	----------DD	2	2	2	►	0	2	0	1-1 (2x)	22	5
27th Nov	Fulham	4 - 3	3	---------LWW	8	5	2	►	2	0	0	3-4 (1x)	30	2
4th Dec	Tottenham	1 - 0	10	LWWWLLD--WLW	10	12	6	►	5	1	0	2-1 (2x)	34	8
11th Dec	C Palace	n/a	3	D-W--W------	6	4	2	►	2	0	0	3-3 (1x)	44	5
18th Dec	Everton	2 - 1	10	LWWLDWL--WLW	15	13	7	►	4	1	2	3-2 (1x)	21	8
26th Dec	Newcastle	1 - 1	9	-WWWWWD--DWD	14	6	6	►	5	1	0	1-0 (4x)	59	6

Home fixture

Date	Opposition	03-04 scoreline	Played	Premiership history	Goals for	Goals against	⚽	▶	W	D	L	Most common score (no. times)	Avg time of first goal (mins)	Avg no. of corners	
28th Dec	Bolton	2 - 2	5	---L-L---DDD	6	8	0	▶	0	0	0	2-1 (2x)	64	6	
1st Jan	Aston Villa	2 - 0	10	DWWLLWW--LLW	11	9	5	▶	5	0	0	2-0 (2x)	26	6	
3rd Jan	Charlton	0 - 1	4	------W--WWL	6	2	3	▶	3	0	0	1-0 (2x)	38	6	🏠
15th Jan	Portsmouth	2 - 1	1	-----------W	2	1	1	▶	1	0	0	1-2 (1x)	35	6	
22nd Jan	Bolton	3 - 4	5	---W-W---DDL	10	7	2	▶	2	0	0	3-1 (2x)	26	8	🏠
2nd Feb	Chelsea	2 - 3	10	WWWWDWL--DLL	18	12	7	▶	4	1	2	2-3 (2x)	21	7	🏠
5th Feb	Middlesbro	1 - 0	7	L--LL-L--WLW	8	11	4	▶	2	0	2	2-1 (2x)	48	5	
12th Feb	Norwich	n/a	3	WLD---------	9	4	2	▶	1	0	1	7-1 (1x)	8	8	🏠
26th Feb	Liverpool	0 - 4	10	LWLLDDL--LDL	7	18	2	▶	1	0	1	2-1 (2x)	52	6	
5th Mar	Everton	1 - 0	10	LWWLWLD--WLW	12	8	7	▶	5	0	2	2-1 (2x)	26	3	
19th Mar	Arsenal	0 - 2	10	WDWDLLL--LWL	12	16	5	▶	3	2	0	1-1 (2x)	38	5	🏠
2nd Apr	Man Utd	1 - 2	10	LDLLDLL--LLL	9	22	3	▶	0	0	1	3-1 (2x)	37	4	
9th Apr	Southampton	1 - 1	10	DWWWWWL--WWD	14	7	7	▶	7	0	0	2-1 (2x)	26	7	🏠
16th Apr	West Brom	n/a	1	----------W-	2	0	1	▶	1	0	0	0-2 (1x)	72	2	
20th Apr	C Palace	n/a	3	L-W--D------	5	5	1	▶	1	0	0	2-2 (1x)	30	9	🏠
23rd Apr	Man City	2 - 3	6	WWLW------WL	10	6	5	▶	4	0	1	2-3 (2x)	26	7	🏠
30th Apr	Birmingham	4 - 0	2	----------WW	5	0	2	▶	2	0	0	0-4 (1x)	40	5	
7th May	Fulham	0 - 2	3	---------WWL	5	3	2	▶	2	0	0	3-0 (1x)	44	4	🏠
14th May	Tottenham	0 - 1	10	WWLWLDL--LWL	14	12	5	▶	4	0	1	2-1 (2x)	30	6	

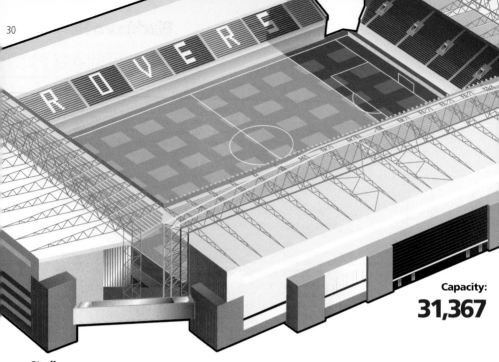

Capacity:

31,367

Stadium:

Ewood Park

Useful Information

Website: **www.rovers.co.uk**
Address: **Ewood Park, Blackburn,
Lancashire BB2 4JF**
Main Switchboard: **08701 113232**

Travel Information

Car Parking: Car parking can be
found immediately adjacent to the
stadium for up to 800 vehicles;
there are three other car parks on
Albion St, Albion Rd and Branch
Rd on the industrial estates.
Street parking is very limited.
By Train: Blackburn station is approx 1.5
miles away, Mill Hill is approx 1 mile away.
By Bus: There are 3 matchday services that
run from Accrington (Route A), Intack
(Route B) and Darwen (Route C).
This service costs £2.00 for a return ticket.
Tickets are not interchangeable between routes.

Seating Plan

CIS Stand		
Blackburn Stand (Lower Tier)	Family Area / Away Fans / Disabled Fans	Darwen End (Lower Tier) / International Suite / Darwen End (Upper Tier)
Jack Walker Stand (Lower Tier)		
Premier Suite / Centenary Suite		
Jack Walker Stand (Upper Tier)		

Area Map

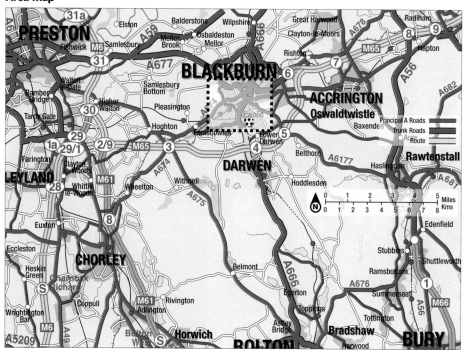

Local Map

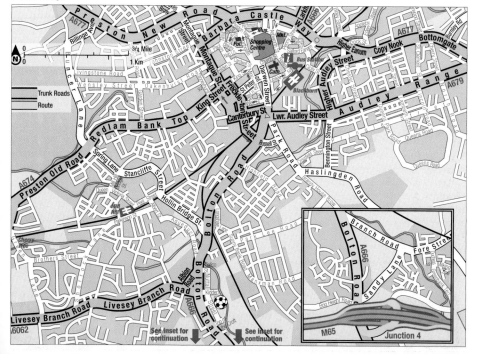

Bolton Wanderers
Manager: **Sam Allardyce**

Club Honours and Records
Division 1: 1996-97
Division 2: 1908-09, 1977-78
Division 3: 1972-73
FA Cup: 1923, 1926, 1929, 1958
Sherpa Van Trophy: 1989

Squad List (stats from 2003-04 season)

Position		Appearances	Apps as Sub	Goals/Clean Sheets	Assists	Yellow Card	Red Card
G	J.Jaaskelainen	38		10		1	
D	A.Barness	11	4				
D	S.Charlton	28	3		2	1	
D	R.Gardner	20	2		1	5	
D	S.Howey	2	1				
D	N.Hunt	28	3	1	2	6	
D	F.Laville	5				1	
D	B.N'Gotty	32	1	3	2	3	
D	J.Otsemobor	1					
D	E.Thome	25	1		1	7	
M	I.Ba		9				
M	I.Campo	37	1	4	3	9	
M	Y.Djorkaeff	24	3	9	5	1	
M	P.Frandsen	22	11	1	1	5	
M	Stelios	17	14	2	3	4	
M	G.Little		4		1		
M	K.Nolan	37		9	2	8	
M	J.Okocha	33	2		8	4	
F	K.Davies	38		9	11	9	
F	D.Facey		1				
F	M.Jardel		7		1	1	
F	J.Moreno	1	7				
F	H.Pedersen	19	14	7	2	1	
F	R.Vaz Te		1				

Five Season Form

Games Won	Games Drawn	Games Lost	Goals For	Goals Against	Goal Difference
38%	**32%**	**30%**	**256**	**264**	**-8**

Ten Season Form

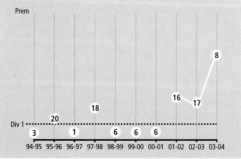

J.Jaaskelainen

R.Gardner
S.Charlton
A.Barness

B.N'Gotty
S.Charlton

E.Thome
B.N'Gotty
F.Laville

N.Hunt
B.N'Gotty

I.Campo

J.Okocha
P.Frandsen

H.Pedersen
Y.Djorkaeff
Stelios

K.Nolan
P.Frandsen

Y.Djorkaeff
K.Nolan
Stelios

K.Davies

Top Goalscorers

9 Goals

	Left Foot	Right Foot	Header
K.Nolan	4	4	1
K.Davies	1	6	2
Y.Djorkaeff	1	7	1

Goal Breakdown

(stats from 2003-04 season)

	Set Piece	Open Play	Total
Kevin Nolan	4	5	9
Kevin Davies	1	8	9
Youri Djorkaeff	2	7	9
Henrik Pedersen	1	6	7
Ivan Campo	1	3	4
Bruno N'Gotty	2	1	3
Stelios	-	2	2
Per Frandsen		1	1
Nicky Hunt	1	-	1

Premiership Statistics

First Goal Scored (average)

Home	Away
28 mins	**29** mins

First Goal Conceded (average)

Home	Away
24 mins	**27** mins

Clean Sheets	Failed To Score
10	**10** matches

Corners Per Game (average)	Average shots on target
6	**5**

Most Common Result:
2-1 (five times)

Most First Goals:
6 - Kevin Nolan

Hat-Tricks:
None

Fastest Goal (mins):
1 - Kevin Nolan v Blackburn (A)
1 - Henrik Pedersen v Charlton (A)

Fastest Booking (mins):
1 - Kevin Davies v Man City (A)

Highest Attendance:
28,353 v Leicester City 28/12/03.

Lowest Attendance:
23,098 v Charlton 30/08/03.

Average Attendance: 26,794

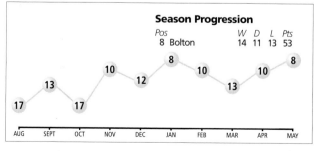

Season Progression

Pos   W   D   L   Pts
8 Bolton   14   11   13   53

17 — 13 — 17 — 10 — 12 — 8 — 10 — 13 — 10 — 8

AUG   SEPT   OCT   NOV   DEC   JAN   FEB   MAR   APR   MAY

Bolton Wanderers

Enhanced Fixture List 2004-05

In this fixture...

Date	Opposition	03-04 scoreline	Played	Premiership history	Goals for	Goals against	No. of times ⚽ ►		W	D	L	Most common score (no. times)	Avg time of first goal (mins)	Avg no. of corners
14th Aug	Charlton	0 - 0	3	---------DLD	1	2	1	►	0	0	1	0-0 (2x)	2	8
21st Aug	Fulham	1 - 2	3	---------LLL	2	9	2	►	0	0	2	4-1 (1x)	29	2
25th Aug	Southampton	2 - 1	5	---L-W---DDW	3	2	1	►	1	0	0	0-0 (2x)	60	4
29th Aug	Liverpool	2 - 2	5	---L-D---WLD	7	8	2	►	1	1	0	2-3 (1x)	44	5
11th Sep	Man Utd	1 - 2	5	---L-D---LDL	2	13	1	►	0	1	0	1-2 (1x)	75	8
18th Sep	Arsenal	1 - 2	5	---L-L---DLL	5	11	2	►	0	0	2	2-1 (3x)	52	1
25th Sep	Birmingham	0 - 1	2	---------WL	4	3	1	►	1	0	0	4-2 (1x)	12	5
2nd Oct	West Brom	n/a	1	---------D-	1	1	1	►	0	1	0	1-1 (1x)	18	4
16th Oct	C Palace	n/a	1	-----W------	5	2	1	►	1	0	0	5-2 (1x)	7	6
23rd Oct	Tottenham	1 - 0	5	---D-L---LLW	6	9	2	►	1	0	1	3-2 (1x)	55	4
31st Oct	Newcastle	1 - 0	5	---L-W---LWW	7	10	3	►	3	0	0	1-0 (2x)	21	7
7th Nov	Middlesbro	0 - 2	4	---W-----DLL	5	6	1	►	1	0	0	2-0 (2x)	43	6
13th Nov	Aston Villa	2 - 2	5	---L-L---WWD	6	7	2	►	2	0	0	3-2 (1x)	37	4
20th Nov	Chelsea	2 - 1	5	---L-L---LLW	5	12	2	►	0	0	2	5-1 (1x)	17	5
27th Nov	Portsmouth	1 - 0	1	---------W	1	0	1	►	1	0	0	1-0 (1x)	53	2
4th Dec	Everton	2 - 1	5	---L-L---LDW	5	10	1	►	1	0	0	3-2 (1x)	44	3
11th Dec	Norwich	n/a	These teams have never played each other in the Premiership											
18th Dec	Man City	1 - 3	3	---D------WL	4	4	2	►	1	0	1	2-0 (1x)	43	7
26th Dec	Man Utd	0 - 4	5	---L-D---WWL	4	9	2	►	1	1	0	4-0 (1x)	57	4

Home fixture

Date	Opposition	03-04 scoreline	Played	Premiership history	Goals for	Goals against	⚽	►	W	D	L	Most common score (no. times)	Avg time of first goal (mins)	Avg no. of corners	
28th Dec	Blackburn	2 - 2	5	---W-W---DDD	8	6	5	►	2	3	0	2-1 (2x)	19	5	👕
1st Jan	West Brom	n/a	1	----------D-	1	1	0	►	0	0	0	1-1 (1x)	89	7	👕
3rd Jan	Birmingham	0 - 2	2	----------LL	1	5	0	►	0	0	0	3-1 (1x)	72	5	
15th Jan	Arsenal	1 - 1	5	---W-L---LDD	4	6	1	►	1	0	0	2-2 (1x)	64	5	👕
22nd Jan	Blackburn	4 - 3	5	---L-L---DDW	7	10	2	►	1	1	0	3-1 (2x)	46	4	
1st Feb	Tottenham	2 - 0	5	---L-D---DWW	7	5	3	►	2	1	0	1-1 (2x)	52	9	👕
5th Feb	C Palace	n/a	1	------D------	2	2	0	►	0	0	0	2-2 (1x)	36	5	
12th Feb	Middlesbro	2 - 0	4	---D-----WWW	6	2	4	►	3	1	0	2-1 (1x)	24	7	👕
26th Feb	Newcastle	0 - 0	5	---L-L---LLD	4	8	1	►	0	0	1	2-1 (2x)	37	3	
5th Mar	Man City	2 - 6	3	---L------LL	2	9	1	►	0	0	1	6-2 (1x)	24	3	
19th Mar	Norwich	n/a		These teams have never played each other in the Premiership											👕
2nd Apr	Liverpool	1 - 3	5	---L-L---DLL	5	13	1	►	0	0	1	5-2 (1x)	62	5	
9th Apr	Fulham	0 - 2	3	---------DDL	0	2	0	►	0	0	0	0-0 (2x)	N/A	6	👕
16th Apr	Charlton	2 - 1	3	---------WDW	5	3	2	►	2	0	0	1-2 (2x)	34	4	
19th Apr	Southampton	0 - 0	5	---L-D---LDD	1	3	0	►	0	0	0	0-1 (2x)	90	8	👕
23rd Apr	Aston Villa	1 - 1	5	---L-W---LLD	6	8	3	►	1	1	1	3-2 (1x)	22	4	
30th Apr	Chelsea	0 - 2	5	---W-W---DDL	6	6	2	►	1	1	0	2-2 (1x)	58	6	👕
7th May	Portsmouth	0 - 4	1	----------L	0	4	0	►	0	0	0	4-0 (1x)	N/A	4	
14th May	Everton	2 - 0	5	---D-D---DLW	6	5	3	►	1	2	0	2-2 (1x)	32	6	👕

Capacity:
28,723

Stadium:
Reebok Stadium

Useful Information
Website: **www.bwfc.co.uk**
Address: **The Reebok Stadium, Burnden Way, Bolton BL6 6JW**
Main Switchboard: **01204 673 673**

Travel Information
Car Parking: Parking is available in the allocated away parking area for £5. Follow signs for car park 'A'. There is also some parking available at British Aerospace for £3, some of which goes to charity. This is past the signs for car park 'A' and right at the next set of traffic lights.
By Train: Horwich Parkway station is a two minute walk from the ground. Bolton station is approx 5 miles away from the Reebok stadium.
By Bus: The club runs buses from Bolton town centre to the ground for £1.30 return. In addition, the number 539 bus runs directly to the ground.

Seating Plan

| East Stand (Upper Tier) |
| East Stand (Lower Tier) |

| North Stand (Upper Tier) | North Stand (Lower Tier) | Family Area / Away Fans / Disabled Fans | South Stand (Lower Tier) | South Stand (Upper Tier) |

| West Stand (Lower Tier) |
| West Stand (Upper Tier) |

Area Map

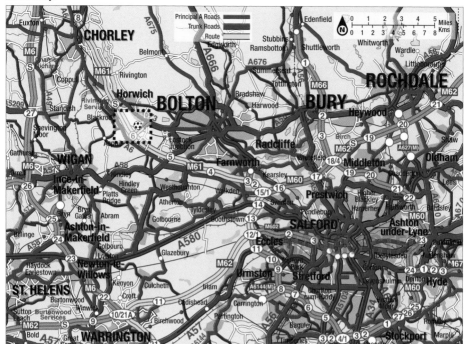

Local Map

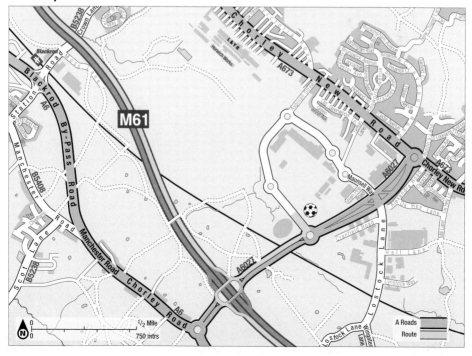

Charlton Athletic

Manager: **Alan Curbishley**

Club Honours and Records

Division 1: 1999-00
Division 3: 1928-29
Div 3 (South): 1934-35
FA Cup: 1947

Squad List (stats from 2003-04 season)

Position		Appearances	Apps as Sub	Goals/Clean Sheets	Assists	Yellow Cards	Red Cards
G	D.Kiely	37		10			
G	S.Royce	1					
D	M.Fish	23				1	1
D	J.Fortune	21	7	2		2	
D	H.Hreidarsson	33		2	2	3	
D	P.Konchesky	17	4		2	3	
D	C.Perry	25	4	1	1	5	
D	C.Powell	11	5		1	1	
D	G.Rowett	1					
D	L.Young	21	3			5	
M	J.Campbell-Ryce		2				
M	M.Holland	38		6	2		
M	C.Jensen	27	4	4	5	1	
M	R.Kishishev	30	3			4	
M	S.Parker	20		2	3	5	1
M	G.Stuart	23	5	3	1		
M	J.Thomas		1				
F	S.Bartlett	13	6	5	2	1	
F	C.Cole	8	13	4			
F	P.Di Canio	23	8	4	15	1	
F	J.Euell	24	7	10	4	3	1
F	J.Johansson	16	10	4	3		
F	K.Lisbie	5	4	4	1		
F	M.Svensson	1	2				

Five Season Form

Games Won	Games Drawn	Games Lost	Goals For	Goals Against	Goal Difference
40%	26%	34%	246	257	-11

Ten Season Form

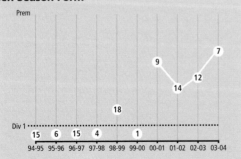

Prem

7

9

12

14

18

Div 1

15 6 15 4 1

94-95 95-96 96-97 97-98 98-99 99-00 00-01 01-02 02-03 03-04

	D.Kiely		H.Hreidarsson	
	S.Royce		C.Powell	

D.Kiely
S.Royce

H.Hreidarsson
C.Powell

M.Fish
H.Hreidarsson

C.Perry
J.Fortune

P.Konchesky
G.Stuart
C.Jensen

L.Young
R.Kishishev

S.Parker
C.Jensen
J.Euell

M.Holland
J.Euell
C.Jensen

R.Kishishev
G.Stuart
M.Holland

J.Euell
S.Bartlett
C.Cole

P.Di Canio
J.Johansson

Top Goalscorer
Jason Euell

10 Goals

	Left Foot	Right Foot	Header
Total	3	7	-

% of team's goals **20%**

Goal Breakdown
(stats from 2003-04 season)

	Set Piece	Open Play	Total
Jason Euell	4	6	**10**
Matt Holland	2	4	**6**
Shaun Bartlett	2	3	**5**
Paolo Di Canio	4	-	**4**
Kevin Lisbie	2	2	**4**
Claus Jensen	3	1	**4**
Jonatan Johansson	-	4	**4**
Carlton Cole	2	2	**4**
Graham Stuart	1	2	**3**
Hermann Hreidarsson	2	-	**2**
Scott Parker	-	2	**2**
Jonathan Fortune	1	1	**2**
Chris Perry	1	-	**1**

Premiership Statistics

First Goal Scored (average)

Home	Away
22 mins	**38** mins

First Goal Conceded (average)

Home	Away
31 mins	**17** mins

Clean Sheets	Failed To Score
10	**9** matches

Corners Per Game (average)	Average shots on target
5	**4**

Most Common Results:
1-0, 1-1 (five times)

Most First Goals:
4 - Jason Euell, Matt Holland

Hat-Tricks:
Kevin Lisbie v Liverpool (H).

Fastest Goal (mins):
1 - Hermann Hreidarsson v Chelsea (H)

Fastest Booking (mins):
13 - Hermann Hreidarsson v Bolton (A)

Highest Attendance:
26,768 v Chelsea 26/12/03

Lowest Attendance:
25,206 v Birmingham 17/04/04

Average Attendance: 26,293

Season Progression

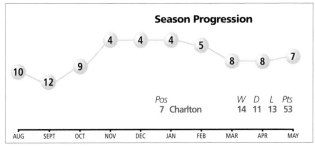

10 · 12 · 9 · 4 · 4 · 4 · 5 · 8 · 8 · 7

| | AUG | SEPT | OCT | NOV | DEC | JAN | FEB | MAR | APR | MAY |

Pos
7 Charlton

W	D	L	Pts
14	11	13	53

Charlton Athletic

Enhanced Fixture List 2004-05

In this fixture...

Date	Opposition	03-04 scoreline	Played	Premiership history	Goals for	Goals against	No. of times Charlton scored first and the result that followed ⚽	►	W	D	L	Most common score (no. times)	Avg time of first goal (mins)	Avg no. corn...
14th Aug	Bolton	0 - 0	3	---------DWD	2	1	0	►	0	0	0	0-0 (2x)	26	4
21st Aug	Portsmouth	1 - 1	1	----------D	1	1	1	►	0	1	0	1-1 (1x)	8	6
24th Aug	Aston Villa	1 - 2	5	------L-DLWL	8	8	3	►	1	1	1	1-2 (2x)	41	6
28th Aug	Man City	1 - 1	3	--------W-WD	6	2	2	►	2	0	0	1-4 (1x)	63	4
13th Sep	Southampton	2 - 1	5	------W-DDWW	11	4	4	►	3	1	0	2-1 (2x)	34	8
18th Sep	Birmingham	2 - 1	2	----------DW	3	2	2	►	1	1	0	1-2 (1x)	24	6
27th Sep	Blackburn	3 - 2	4	------D--LWW	6	5	2	►	2	0	0	3-2 (1x)	35	7
2nd Oct	Arsenal	1 - 2	5	------D-LWLL	8	11	0	►	0	0	0	5-3 (1x)	39	4
17th Oct	Newcastle	0 - 0	5	------D-WDLD	5	5	1	►	1	0	0	2-2 (1x)	61	6
23rd Oct	Liverpool	1 - 0	5	------D-LLLW	5	10	3	►	1	1	1	3-3 (1x)	45	5
30th Oct	Middlesbro	1 - 0	5	------D-WDWW	4	1	4	►	3	1	0	1-0 (3x)	34	5
6th Nov	Tottenham	1 - 0	5	------D-DWDW	6	4	4	►	2	2	0	2-2 (2x)	46	5
13th Nov	Norwich	n/a		These teams have never played each other in the Premiership										
20th Nov	Man Utd	0 - 2	5	------L-LDLL	3	12	1	►	0	0	1	4-1 (2x)	36	3
27th Nov	Chelsea	4 - 2	5	------L-WWLW	10	7	4	►	3	0	1	4-2 (1x)	29	5
5th Dec	C Palace	n/a		These teams have never played each other in the Premiership										
11th Dec	West Brom	n/a	1	----------W-	1	0	1	►	1	0	0	0-1 (1x)	60	6
20th Dec	Fulham	3 - 1	3	---------DLW	4	3	2	►	1	1	0	3-1 (1x)	22	3
26th Dec	Southampton	2 - 3	5	------L-DLDL	3	7	0	►	0	0	0	0-0 (2x)	30	5

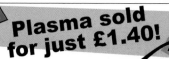

Home fixture

Date	Opposition	03-04 scoreline	Played	Premiership history	Goals for	Goals against	⚽ No. of times Charlton scored first	►	W	D	L	Most common score (no. times)	Avg time of first goal (mins)	Avg no. of corners	Home fixture
28th Dec	Everton	2 - 2	5	------L-WLWD	7	7	4	►	2	1	1	1-2 (2x)	36	7	
1st Jan	Arsenal	1 - 1	5	------L-WLLD	2	8	2	►	1	1	0	0-3 (2x)	34	5	
3rd Jan	Blackburn	1 - 0	4	------L--LLW	2	6	1	►	1	0	0	1-0 (2x)	42	6	
15th Jan	Birmingham	1 - 1	2	----------LD	1	3	0	►	0	0	0	1-1 (1x)	86	9	👕
22nd Jan	Everton	1 - 0	5	------L-LWLW	5	8	2	►	2	0	0	4-1 (1x)	50	5	
1st Feb	Liverpool	3 - 2	5	------W-LLWW	6	8	2	►	2	0	0	3-2 (1x)	46	8	👕
5th Feb	Newcastle	1 - 3	5	------D-WLLL	3	8	2	►	1	0	1	3-1 (1x)	31	5	
12th Feb	Tottenham	2 - 4	5	------L-WWLL	7	10	3	►	2	0	1	3-1 (1x)	25	8	👕
26th Feb	Middlesbro	0 - 0	5	------L-DDDD	1	3	1	►	0	1	0	0-0 (3x)	26	6	
5th Mar	Fulham	0 - 2	3	---------DLL	0	3	0	►	0	0	0	2-0 (1x)	N/A	8	
19th Mar	West Brom	n/a	1	----------W-	1	0	1	►	1	0	0	1-0 (1x)	6	6	👕
2nd Apr	Man City	0 - 3	3	--------W-DL	6	5	2	►	1	0	0	4-0 (1x)	31	5	👕
9th Apr	Portsmouth	2 - 1	1	-----------W	2	1	0	►	0	0	0	1-2 (1x)	77	9	
16th Apr	Bolton	1 - 2	3	---------LDL	3	5	1	►	0	1	0	1-2 (2x)	37	5	👕
20th Apr	Aston Villa	1 - 2	5	------W-LLLL	6	10	1	►	1	0	0	2-1 (2x)	57	3	
23rd Apr	Norwich	n/a		These teams have never played each other in the Premiership											
30th Apr	Man Utd	0 - 2	5	------L-DLLL	4	11	2	►	0	1	1	0-2 (2x)	27	5	👕
7th May	Chelsea	0 - 1	5	------L-WWLL	4	7	2	►	2	0	0	0-1 (2x)	56	3	
14th May	C Palace	n/a		These teams have never played each other in the Premiership												👕

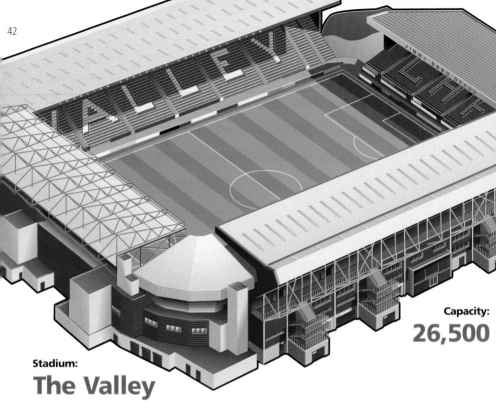

Capacity:
26,500

Stadium:
The Valley

Useful Information
Website: www.cafc.co.uk
Address: The Valley, Floyd Road, Charlton, London SE7 8BL
Main Switchboard: 020 8333 4000

Travel Information
Car Parking: Parking is available on Victoria Way, an 8 minute walk from the ground. It costs £5 and payment is on the gate. Street parking is very limited around the ground and public transport is recommended.

By Train: Trains run from Charing Cross, London Bridge and Waterloo East to Charlton station, approx 2 minutes walk. Turn right out of station and the left into Floyd Road. North Greenwich on the Jubilee Line has bus links to the ground.

By Bus: Numbers 177 (towards Peckham), 180 (towards Lewisham), 53 (towards Plumstead) or 54 (toward Woolwich). 161, 422, 472, 486 (towards North Greenwich).

Seating Plan

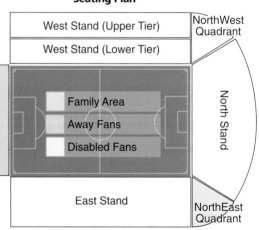

West Stand (Upper Tier)
West Stand (Lower Tier)
NorthWest Quadrant
South Stand
Family Area
Away Fans
Disabled Fans
North Stand
East Stand
NorthEast Quadrant

Area Map

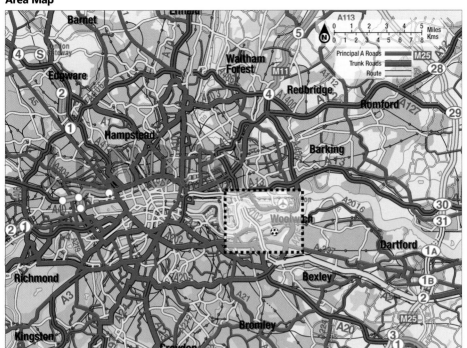

Local Map

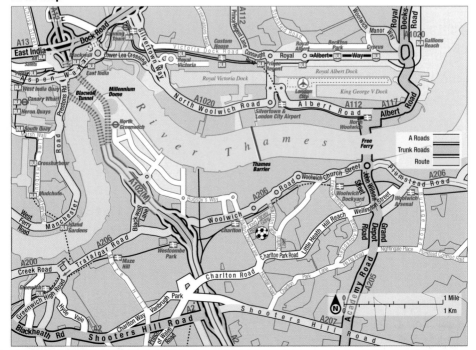

Chelsea
Manager: **Jose Mourinho**

Club Honours and Records
Football League: 1954-55
Division 2: 1983-84, 1988-89
FA Cup: 1970, 1997, 2000
League Cup: 1965, 1998
Full Members Cup: 1986
Zenith Data Systems Cup: 1990
European Super Cup: 1998
Cup-Winners Cup: 1970-71, 1997-98

Five Season Form

Games Won	Games Drawn	Games Lost	Goals For	Goals Against	Goal Difference
50%	**27%**	**23%**	**210**	**185**	**+25**

Ten Season Form
Prem

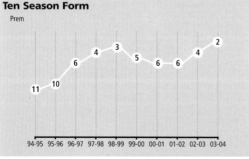

94-95 95-96 96-97 97-98 98-99 99-00 00-01 01-02 02-03 03-04

Squad List (stats from 2003-04 season)

Position		Appearances	Apps as Sub	Goals/Clean Sheets	Assists	Yellow Cards	Red Cards
G	M.Ambrosio	8		4			
G	C.Cudicini	26		14			
G	N.Sullivan	4		3			
D	C.Babayaro	5	1	1	2		
D	W.Bridge	33		1	4		
D	M.Desailly	15			1		
D	W.Gallas	23	6			1	
D	R.Huth	8	8			6	1
D	G.Johnson	17	2	3	1	3	
D	M.Melchiot	20	3	2		1	
D	J.Terry	33		2	2	5	
M	J.Cole	18	17	1	6	3	
M	D.Duff	17	6	5	9		
M	Geremi	19	6	1	4		1
M	J.Gronkjaer	19	12	2	3	5	
M	F.Lampard	38		10	7	3	
M	C.Makelele	26	4		2	2	
M	A.Nicolas	1	1				
M	S.Parker	7	4	1		2	
M	E.Petit	3	1		1		
M	M.Stanic		2				
M	J.Veron	5	2	1	1		
F	H.Crespo	13	6	10		1	
F	E.Gudjohnsen	17	9	6	2		1
F	J.Hasselbaink	22	8	12	10	6	
F	A.Mutu	21	4	6	8	5	

C.Cudicini
M.Ambrosio
N.Sullivan

W.Bridge
C.Babayaro

J.Terry
M.Desailly
R.Huth

W.Gallas
J.Terry
M.Desailly

D.Duff
J.Cole
Geremi

M.Melchiot
G.Johnson
W.Gallas

F.Lampard

C.Makelele
Geremi
S.Parker

J.Gronkjaer
Geremi
D.Duff

J.Hasselbaink
E.Gudjohnsen

A.Mutu
H.Crespo

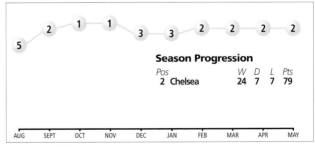

Top Goalscorer
Jimmy Floyd Hasselbaink

12 Goals

	Left Foot	Right Foot	Header
Total	2	10	-

% of team's goals **18%**

Goal Breakdown
(stats from 2003-04 season)

	Set Piece	Open Play	Total
J-F Hasselbaink	2	10	**12**
Frank Lampard	2	8	**10**
Hernan Crespo	1	9	**10**
Eidur Gudjohnsen	-	6	**6**
Adrian Mutu	1	5	**6**
Damien Duff	-	5	**5**
Glen Johnson	1	2	**3**
John Terry	1	1	**2**
Mario Melchiot	-	2	**2**
Jesper Gronkjaer	1	1	**2**
Celestine Babayaro	-	1	**1**
Scott Parker	-	1	**1**
Wayne Bridge	-	1	**1**
Joe Cole	-	1	**1**
Juan Sebastian Veron	-	1	**1**
Geremi	-	1	**1**

Premiership Statistics

First Goal Scored (average)

Home
22
mins

Away
31
mins

First Goal Conceded (average)

Home
10
mins

Away
16
mins

Clean Sheets
21

Failed To Score
5
matches

Corners Per Game (average)
6

Average shots on target
5

Most Common Result:
1-0 (ten times)

Most First Goals:
5 - Frank Lampard, Jimmy Floyd Hasselbaink

Hat-Tricks:
Jimmy Floyd Hasselbaink v Wolves (H)

Fastest Goal (mins):
1 - Eidur Gudjohnsen v Arsenal (H)

Fastest Booking (mins):
8 - Jesper Gronkjaer v Charlton (H)

Highest Attendance:
41,932 v Man Utd 30/11/03

Lowest Attendance:
40,491 v Bolton 13/12/03

Average Attendance: 41,234

Season Progression

5 2 1 1 3 3 2 2 2 2

Pos
2 Chelsea

	W	D	L	Pts
	24	7	7	79

AUG SEPT OCT NOV DEC JAN FEB MAR APR MAY

Chelsea

Enhanced Fixture List 2004-05

In this fixture...

	Date	Opposition	03-04 scoreline	Played	Premiership history	Goals for	Goals against	No. of times Chelsea scored first ⚽	►	W	D	L	Most common score (no. times)	Avg time of first goal (mins)	Avg no. of corners
👕	15th Aug	Man Utd	1 - 0	12	DWLLDLDWDLDW	15	16	7	►	3	4	0	1-1 (3x)	31	6
	21st Aug	Birmingham	0 - 0	2	----------WD	3	1	1	►	1	0	0	1-3 (1x)	44	10
	24th Aug	C Palace	n/a	3	D-W--W------	5	1	3	►	2	1	0	1-1 (1x)	25	5
👕	28th Aug	Southampton	4 - 0	12	DWLWWWWDWLDW	20	10	7	►	7	0	0	1-0 (3x)	44	6
	11th Sep	Aston Villa	2 - 3	12	WLLWWWWDDDLL	16	12	5	►	4	0	1	1-1 (2x)	52	4
👕	19th Sep	Tottenham	4 - 2	12	DWDDWWWWWWDW	26	9	6	►	6	0	0	1-1 (3x)	49	7
	25th Sep	Middlesbro	2 - 1	9	D--LL-DWLWDW	6	6	3	►	3	0	0	1-0 (2x)	38	7
👕	3rd Oct	Liverpool	0 - 1	12	DWDDWWWWWWWL	21	6	8	►	7	1	0	2-1 (2x)	16	4
	16th Oct	Man City	1 - 0	7	WDWW----W-WW	12	4	6	►	5	1	0	0-1 (3x)	44	4
👕	23rd Oct	Blackburn	2 - 2	10	DLLLDLD--DLD	9	14	3	►	0	1	2	1-2 (3x)	54	5
	30th Oct	West Brom	n/a	1	----------W-	2	0	1	►	1	0	0	0-2 (1x)	38	4
👕	6th Nov	Everton	0 - 0	12	WWLDDWWDWWWD	23	10	8	►	6	2	0	2-1 (2x)	32	7
	13th Nov	Fulham	1 - 0	3	---------DDW	2	1	2	►	1	1	0	1-1 (1x)	47	6
👕	20th Nov	Bolton	1 - 2	5	---W-W---WWL	12	5	3	►	2	0	1	5-1 (1x)	42	4
	27th Nov	Charlton	2 - 4	5	------W-LLWL	7	10	1	►	1	0	0	4-2 (1x)	37	5
👕	4th Dec	Newcastle	5 - 0	11	-WDWDWDWWDWW	19	5	10	►	6	4	0	1-1 (4x)	30	6
	12th Dec	Arsenal	1 - 2	12	LLLDDLLLDLLL	12	23	4	►	0	2	2	2-1 (4x)	45	4
👕	18th Dec	Norwich	n/a	3	LLW---------	5	5	2	►	1	0	1	2-3 (1x)	43	5
👕	26th Dec	Aston Villa	1 - 0	12	LDWLDLWWWLWW	12	10	7	►	6	0	1	1-0 (4x)	44	6

Home fixture

Date	Opposition	03-04 scoreline	Played	Premiership history	Goals for ⚽	Goals against	No. of times Chelsea scored first ►	W	D	L	Most common score (no. times)	Avg. time of first goal (mins)	Avg no. of corners
28th Dec	Portsmouth	2 - 0	1	----------W	2	0	1 ►	1	0	0	0-2 (1x)	17	10	
1st Jan	Liverpool	2 - 1	12	LLLLLLDLDLLW	11	25	3 ►	1	1	1	1-0 (3x)	35	4	
3rd Jan	Middlesbro	0 - 0	9	W--WW-WDWDWD	18	4	8 ►	6	2	0	1-0 (2x)	39	7	
15th Jan	Tottenham	1 - 0	12	WDDDWWDWWWDW	22	9	10 ►	7	3	0	1-2 (2x)	34	4	
22nd Jan	Portsmouth	3 - 0	1	----------W	3	0	1 ►	1	0	0	3-0 (1x)	65	7	▮
2nd Feb	Blackburn	3 - 2	10	LLLLDLW--DWW	12	18	2 ►	1	0	1	2-3 (2x)	33	5	
5th Feb	Man City	1 - 0	7	LDWD----W-WW	14	6	5 ►	4	1	0	5-0 (1x)	34	5	▮
12th Feb	Everton	1 - 0	12	WLDDWLDDLDWW	16	16	8 ►	4	2	2	1-1 (2x)	36	4	
26th Feb	West Brom	n/a	1	----------W-	2	0	1 ►	1	0	0	2-0 (1x)	30	5	▮
5th Mar	Norwich	n/a	3	LDL---------	2	6	2 ►	0	1	1	3-0 (1x)	29	7	
19th Mar	C Palace	n/a	3	W-D--W------	9	3	1 ►	1	0	0	6-2 (1x)	10	3	▮
2nd Apr	Southampton	1 - 0	12	LLWWDLWWLWDW	15	12	5 ►	5	0	0	1-0 (2x)	46	4	
9th Apr	Birmingham	0 - 0	2	----------WD	3	0	1 ►	1	0	0	3-0 (1x)	3	7	▮
16th Apr	Man Utd	1 - 1	12	LWDDWDDLDWLD	17	17	8 ►	3	4	1	1-1 (3x)	34	3	
20th Apr	Arsenal	1 - 2	12	WLWWLLDLDDDL	13	18	8 ►	3	2	3	2-3 (2x)	36	6	▮
23rd Apr	Fulham	2 - 1	3	--------WDW	6	4	3 ►	2	1	0	3-2 (1x)	21	7	▮
30th Apr	Bolton	2 - 0	5	---L-L---DDW	6	6	3 ►	1	1	1	2-2 (1x)	57	6	
7th May	Charlton	1 - 0	5	------W-LLWW	7	4	3 ►	3	0	0	0-1 (2x)	16	7	▮
14th May	Newcastle	1 - 2	11	-DLLLLWWDWLL	10	17	4 ►	3	0	1	3-1 (2x)	37	4	

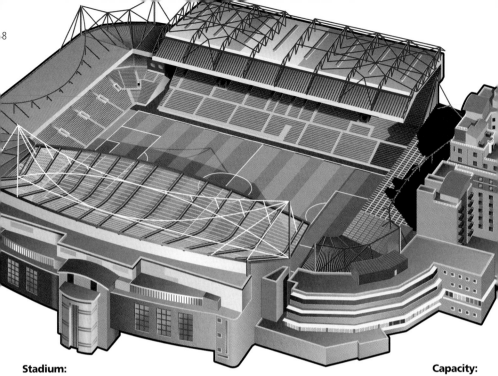

Stadium:

Stamford Bridge

Capacity:

42,449

Useful Information

Website: www.chelseafc.com
Address: **Stamford Bridge, Fulham Road, London SW6 1HS**
Main Switchboard: **020 7385 5545**

Travel Information

Car Parking: Parking restrictions during the game make it advisable to travel by tube. Limited on-site matchday underground parking is available in advance: 0207 915 1956
By Tube: Fulham Broadway is on the District Line, approx 5 minutes walk. Turn left out of station and ground is on the left hand side.
By Bus: Numbers 14 (towards Tottenham Court Road), 414 and 211 (towards Hammersmith) go along Fulham Road. Numbers 11, 14, 28, 211, 295, 391, 414, 424 all stop near the ground.

Seating Plan

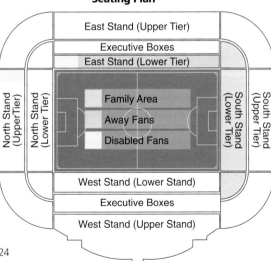

East Stand (Upper Tier)

Executive Boxes

East Stand (Lower Tier)

North Stand (UpperTier)

North Stand (Lower Tier)

Family Area

Away Fans

Disabled Fans

South Stand (Lower Tier)

South Stand (Upper Tier)

West Stand (Lower Stand)

Executive Boxes

West Stand (Upper Stand)

Area Map

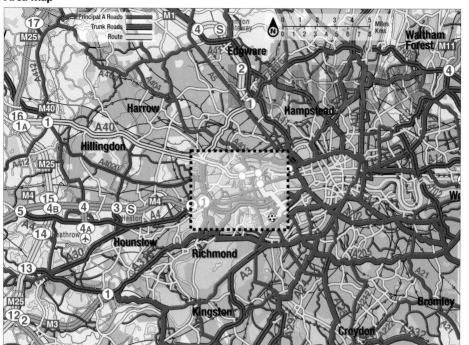

Local Map

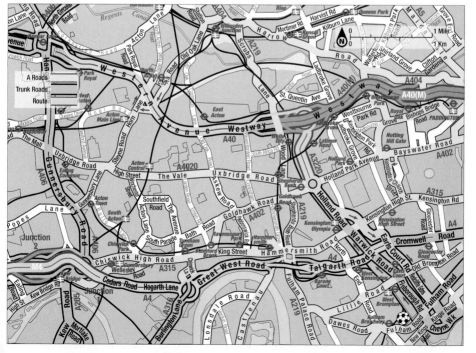

Crystal Palace

Manager: **Iain Dowie**

Club Honours and Records

Division 1: 1993-94
Division 2: 1978-79
Division 3 (South): 1920-21
Zenith Data Systems Cup: 1991

Five Season Form

Games Won	Games Drawn	Games Lost	Goals For	Goals Against	Goal Difference
35%	26%	39%	273	312	-39

Ten Season Form

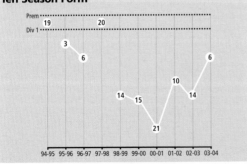

94-95 95-96 96-97 97-98 98-99 99-00 00-01 01-02 02-03 03-04

Squad List (stats from 2003-04 season)

Position		Appearances	Apps as Sub	Goals/Clean Sheets	Assists	Yellow Cards	Red Cards
G	C.Berthelin	17		2			
G	M.Clarke	4		1			
G	T.Myhre	15		5			
G	N.Vaesen	10		5			
D	G.Borrowdale	14	9			3	
D	R.Edwards	6	1	1		1	
D	C.Fleming	15	2		1	3	
D	D.Granville	21		3	5	3	
D	M.Hudson	14			1		1
D	M.Leigertwood	7	5		1	1	
D	T.Popovic	34		1	1	10	
D	D.Powell	10					1
D	J.Smith	13	2		1	3	
D	K.Symons	12	3			1	1
M	T.Black	12	13		5	2	1
M	D.Butterfield	45		4	4	3	
M	S.Derry	25	12	2	3	7	1
M	J.Gray	24		3	4	3	
M	G.Heeroo		1				
M	M.Hughes	34		3	4	10	1
M	H.Mullins	10				5	
M	A.Riihilahti	24	7		1	7	
M	W.Routledge	32	12	6	5	1	1
M	T.Soares		3				
M	B.Watson	8	8	1	1	3	
F	D.Freedman	20	15	13	3	1	
F	A.Johnson	40	2	27	15	4	
F	N.Shipperley	40		8	7	5	

For all statistics, Play-Off matches not included.

C.Berthelin
T.Myhre
N.Vaesen
M.Clarke

D.Granville
G.Borrowdale
H.Mullins

T.Popovic
K.Symons

M.Hudson
D.Powell
M.Leigertwood

J.Gray
W.Routledge

D.Butterfield
C.Fleming
J.Smith

M.Hughes
A.Riihilahti

A.Riihilahti
S.Derry
B.Watson

W.Routledge
D.Butterfield

A.Johnson
D.Freedman

N.Shipperley
D.Freedman

Top Goalscorer
Andy Johnson

27 Goals

	Left Foot	Right Foot	Header
Total	5	19	3

% of team's goals **38%**

Goal Breakdown
(stats from 2003-04 season)

	Set Piece	Open Play	Total
Andy Johnson	8	19	27
Dougie Freedman	4	9	13
Neil Shipperley	1	7	8
Wayne Routledge	1	5	6
Danny Butterfield	1	3	4
Danny Granville	2	1	3
Michael Hughes	-	3	3
Julian Gray	-	3	3
Shaun Derry	-	2	2
Tony Popovic		1	1
Rob Edwards	1	-	1
Ben Watson	1	-	1

League Statistics

First Goal Scored (average)

Home	Away
39 mins	**31** mins

First Goal Conceded (average)

Home	Away
25 mins	**33** mins

Clean Sheets	Failed To Score
13	**8** matches

Corners Per Game (average)	Average shots on target
6	**5**

Most Common Result:
1-0 (seven times)

Most First Goals:
17 - Andy Johnson

Hat-Tricks:
Andy Johnson v Crewe (A),
Andy Johnson v Stoke (H),
Dougie Freedman v Burnley (A).

Fastest Goal (mins):
2 - Shaun Derry v Norwich (A)

Fastest Booking (mins):
3 - Tommy Black v Sheff Utd (H)

Highest Attendance:
23,977 v West Ham 12/04/04.

Lowest Attendance:
12,259 v Crewe 09/12/03.

Average Attendance: 17,344

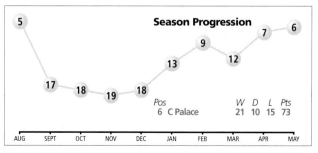

Season Progression

5, 17, 18, 19, 18, 13, 9, 12, 7, 6

AUG SEPT OCT NOV DEC JAN FEB MAR APR MAY

Pos		W	D	L	Pts
6	C Palace	21	10	15	73

Crystal Palace

Enhanced Fixture List 2004-05

In this fixture...

Date	Opposition	03-04 scoreline	Played	Premiership history	Goals for	Goals against	No. of times Crystal Palace scored first ⚽	▶ W	D	L	Most common score (no. times)	Avg time of first goal (mins)	Avg no. corn.
14th Aug	Norwich	n/a	2	L-D---------	2	4	1 ▶	0	0	1	4-2 (1x)	2	7
21st Aug	Everton	n/a	3	L-W--L------	2	5	1 ▶	1	0	0	1-3 (1x)	35	7
24th Aug	Chelsea	n/a	3	D-L--L------	1	5	0 ▶	0	0	0	1-1 (1x)	41	5
28th Aug	Middlesbro	n/a	1	W-----------	1	0	1 ▶	1	0	0	0-1 (1x)	63	1
11th Sep	Portsmouth	n/a		These teams have never played each other in the Premiership									
18th Sep	Man City	n/a	2	D-W---------	2	1	1 ▶	1	0	0	2-1 (1x)	34	9
25th Sep	Aston Villa	n/a	3	L-D--L------	2	7	0 ▶	0	0	0	3-1 (1x)	74	6
2nd Oct	Fulham	n/a		These teams have never played each other in the Premiership									
16th Oct	Bolton	n/a	1	-----L------	2	5	0 ▶	0	0	0	5-2 (1x)	8	6
23rd Oct	West Brom	n/a		These teams have never played each other in the Premiership									
30th Oct	Birmingham	n/a		These teams have never played each other in the Premiership									
6th Nov	Arsenal	n/a	3	L-L--D------	1	5	0 ▶	0	0	0	1-2 (1x)	69	7
13th Nov	Liverpool	n/a	3	L-D--L------	1	7	0 ▶	0	0	0	5-0 (1x)	72	5
20th Nov	Newcastle	n/a	2	--L--L------	1	3	0 ▶	0	0	0	1-2 (1x)	67	5
27th Nov	Southampton	n/a	3	L-L--L------	1	5	0 ▶	0	0	0	1-0 (2x)	27	5
5th Dec	Charlton	n/a		These teams have never played each other in the Premiership									
11th Dec	Blackburn	n/a	3	D-L--L------	4	6	1 ▶	0	1	0	3-3 (1x)	44	5
18th Dec	Man Utd	n/a	3	L-L--L------	0	6	0 ▶	0	0	0	3-0 (1x)	N/A	5
26th Dec	Portsmouth	n/a		These teams have never played each other in the Premiership									

Home fixture

Date	Opposition	03-04 scoreline	Played	Premiership history	Goals for	Goals against	No. of times Crystal Palace scored first ⚽	►	W	D	L	Most common score (no. times)	Avg time of first goal (mins)	Avg no. of corners	
28th Dec	Tottenham	n/a	3	D-D--W------	3	2	1	►	1	0	0	2-2 (1x)	39	5	
1st Jan	Fulham	n/a		These teams have never played each other in the Premiership											
3rd Jan	Aston Villa	n/a	3	W-D--D------	2	1	2	►	1	1	0	1-1 (1x)	26	5	👕
15th Jan	Man City	n/a	2	D-D---------	1	1	0	►	0	0	0	1-1 (1x)	31	6	
22nd Jan	Tottenham	n/a	3	L-D--L------	3	7	1	►	0	1	0	1-3 (2x)	59	5	👕
1st Feb	West Brom	n/a		These teams have never played each other in the Premiership											
5th Feb	Bolton	n/a	1	-----D------	2	2	1	►	0	1	0	2-2 (1x)	9	4	👕
12th Feb	Arsenal	n/a	3	L-W--L------	2	5	1	►	1	0	0	3-0 (1x)	19	5	
26th Feb	Birmingham	n/a		These teams have never played each other in the Premiership											👕
5th Mar	Man Utd	n/a	3	L-D--L------	1	6	0	►	0	0	0	1-1 (1x)	79	5	👕
19th Mar	Chelsea	n/a	3	L-D--L------	3	9	1	►	0	0	1	6-2 (1x)	39	8	
2nd Apr	Middlesbro	n/a	1	W-----------	4	1	1	►	1	0	0	4-1 (1x)	54	5	👕
9th Apr	Everton	n/a	3	W-L--W------	5	4	2	►	2	0	0	3-1 (1x)	41	4	
16th Apr	Norwich	n/a	2	L-L---------	1	3	0	►	0	0	0	1-2 (1x)	20	6	👕
20th Apr	Blackburn	n/a	3	W-L--D------	5	5	2	►	1	1	0	2-2 (1x)	31	2	
23rd Apr	Liverpool	n/a	3	D-L--L------	2	10	0	►	0	0	0	1-6 (1x)	64	8	👕
30th Apr	Newcastle	n/a	2	--L--W------	4	4	1	►	1	0	0	3-2 (1x)	33	2	
7th May	Southampton	n/a	3	L-D--D------	2	3	0	►	0	0	0	1-2 (1x)	58	6	👕
14th May	Charlton	n/a		These teams have never played each other in the Premiership											

Capacity:
26,400

Stadium:
Selhurst Park

Useful Information
Website: www.cpfc.co.uk
Address: Selhurst Park, South Norwood,
London SE25 6PU

Travel Information
Car Parking: There is limited car parking at the ground. The best area is Selhurst station. The roads in Thornton Heath are mostly pay-and-display.
By Train: Thornton Heath, Selhurst and Norwood Junction stations are all a five-minute walk from the ground. Trains run from Victoria or London Bridge.
By Bus: Numbers 468, 196 and 410.

Seating Plan

Arthur Wait Stand

Whitehorse Lane Stand

Executive Boxes

Family Area

Away Fans

Disabled Fans

Lower Tier

Upper Tier

Gallery

Holmesdale Road

Main Stand

Area Map

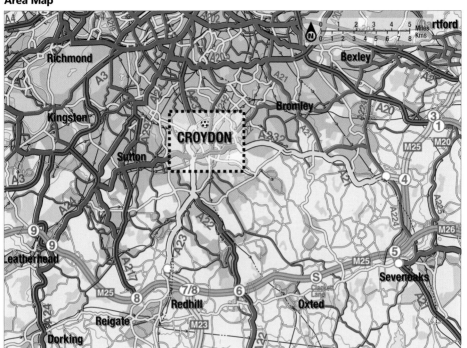

Local Map

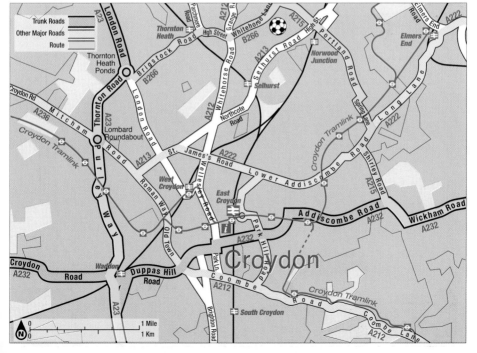

Everton

Manager: David Moyes

Club Honours and Records
Football League: 1890-91, 1914-15, 1927-28, 1931-32, 1938-39, 1962-63, 1969-70, 1984-85, 1986-87
Division 2: 1930-31
FA Cup: 1906, 1933, 1966, 1984, 1995
Cup-Winners Cup: 1984-85

Five Season Form

Games Won	Games Drawn	Games Lost	Goals For	Goals Against	Goal Difference
32%	28%	40%	215	271	-56

Ten Season Form

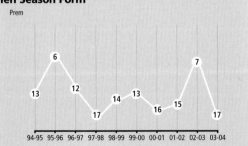

Prem

6
13
12
14
13
17
16
15
7
17

94-95 95-96 96-97 97-98 98-99 99-00 00-01 01-02 02-03 03-04

Squad List (stats from 2003-04 season)

Position		Appearances	Apps as Sub	Goals/Clean Sheets	Assists	Yellow Cards	Red Cards
G	N.Martyn	33	1	10			
G	S.Simonsen	1					
G	R.Wright	4					
D	P.Clarke	1					
D	T.Hibbert	24	1		1	1	
D	A.Pistone	20	1			1	
D	A.Stubbs	25	2			2	
D	D.Unsworth	22	4	3	2	3	
D	S.Watson	22	2	5	3	4	
D	D.Weir	9	1			1	
D	J.Yobo	27	1	2			
M	L.Carsley	15	6	2		4	
M	T.Gravesen	29	1	2	4	5	
M	K.Kilbane	26	4	3	1	1	
M	T.Linderoth	23	4		4	4	
M	G.Naysmith	27	2	2	6	2	1
M	A.Nyarko	7	4			1	
M	L.Osman	3	1	1	1		
M	M.Pembridge	4			2		
M	L.Tie	4	1				1
F	K.Campbell	8	9	1	1	1	
F	N.Chadwick	1	2				
F	D.Ferguson	13	7	5	3	4	1
F	F.Jeffers	5	13		2	2	
F	J.McFadden	11	12		3	3	
F	T.Radzinski	28	6	8	6	2	
F	W.Rooney	26	8	9	4	10	

Formation and Line-ups

N.Martyn
R.Wright
S.Simonsen

G.Naysmith
D.Unsworth

A.Stubbs
D.Unsworth
D.Weir

J.Yobo
A.Stubbs

T.Hibbert
A.Pistone

K.Kilbane
J.McFadden
G.Naysmith

T.Linderoth
L.Carsley

T.Gravesen
L.Carsley
A.Nyarko

S.Watson
J.McFadden
W.Rooney

T.Radzinski
D.Ferguson
F.Jeffers

W.Rooney
D.Ferguson
K.Campbell

Top Goalscorer
Wayne Rooney

9 Goals

	Left Foot	Right Foot	Header
Total	**2**	**7**	**-**

% of team's goals **20%**

Goal Breakdown
(stats from 2003-04 season)

	Set Piece	Open Play	Total
Wayne Rooney	3	6	**9**
Tomasz Radzinski	2	6	**8**
Steve Watson	1	4	**5**
Duncan Ferguson	1	4	**5**
David Unsworth	2	1	**3**
Kevin Kilbane	1	2	**3**
Lee Carsley	1	1	**2**
Thomas Gravesen	-	2	**2**
Gary Naysmith	1	1	**2**
Joseph Yobo	2	-	**2**
Kevin Campbell	1	-	**1**
Leon Osman	-	1	**1**

Premiership Statistics

First Goal Scored (average)

Home	Away
35 mins	**24** mins

First Goal Conceded (average)

Home	Away
31 mins	**26** mins

Clean Sheets	Failed To Score
10	**13** matches

Corners Per Game (average)	Average shots on target
6	**5**

Most Common Result:
0-0, 1-2 (five times)

Most First Goals:
7 - Tomasz Radzinski

Hat-Tricks:
Steve Watson v Leeds United (H)

Fastest Goal (mins):
3 - Leon Osman v Wolves (A)

Fastest Booking (mins):
2 - Gary Naysmith v Liverpool (H)

Highest Attendance:
40,228 v Newcastle 13/09/03

Lowest Attendance:
35,775 v Southampton 19/10/03

Average Attendance: 38,837

Season Progression

Pos		W	D	L	Pts
17 Everton		9	12	17	39

AUG 13 — SEPT 10 — OCT 13 — NOV 18 — DEC 11 — JAN 14 — FEB 14 — MAR 13 — APR 13 — MAY 17

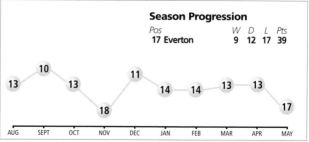

Everton

Enhanced Fixture List 2004-05

In this fixture...

	Date	Opposition	03-04 scoreline	Played	Premiership history	Goals for	Goals against	No. of times Everton scored first ⚽	►	W	D	L	Most common score (no. times)	Avg time of first goal (mins)	Avg no. o...
	15th Aug	Arsenal	1 - 1	12	DDDLLDLLWLWD	9	14	2	►	1	1	0	1-1 (3x)	49	4
	21st Aug	C Palace	n/a	3	W-L--W------	5	2	2	►	2	0	0	1-3 (1x)	27	6
	25th Aug	Man Utd	2 - 3	12	WLLLDLLLLLLL	10	28	3	►	1	1	1	2-0 (3x)	41	3
	28th Aug	West Brom	n/a	1	----------W-	1	0	1	►	1	0	0	1-0 (1x)	35	10
	11th Sep	Man City	1 - 5	7	WLLW----L-LL	9	20	2	►	2	0	0	5-1 (1x)	38	7
	18th Sep	Middlesbro	1 - 1	9	D--WL-WLDWWD	19	10	6	►	3	2	1	2-2 (2x)	30	6
	26th Sep	Portsmouth	2 - 1	1	----------W	2	1	0	►	0	0	0	1-2 (1x)	27	10
	2nd Oct	Tottenham	3 - 1	12	LLDDWLLDDDDW	11	13	5	►	2	3	0	2-2 (2x)	27	7
	16th Oct	Southampton	0 - 0	12	WWDWWWLWWDWWD	22	7	6	►	6	0	0	2-1 (2x)	41	9
	23rd Oct	Norwich	n/a	3	DLD---------	1	4	1	►	0	1	0	3-0 (1x)	55	3
	30th Oct	Aston Villa	2 - 0	12	WLDWLLDDLWWW	12	12	5	►	4	1	0	0-1 (3x)	56	6
	6th Nov	Chelsea	0 - 0	12	LLWDDLLDLLLD	10	23	2	►	1	0	1	2-1 (2x)	46	4
	13th Nov	Birmingham	0 - 3	2	----------DL	1	4	0	►	0	0	0	3-0 (1x)	45	8
	20th Nov	Fulham	3 - 1	3	---------WWW	7	2	3	►	3	0	0	3-1 (1x)	18	4
	28th Nov	Newcastle	2 - 4	11	-LLLLLWDWLLL	11	23	5	►	2	0	3	1-0 (3x)	26	4
	4th Dec	Bolton	1 - 2	5	---W-W---WDL	10	5	3	►	3	0	0	3-2 (1x)	37	7
	11th Dec	Liverpool	0 - 3	12	WWWDDWDDLLLL	14	14	5	►	3	1	1	2-0 (3x)	42	4
	18th Dec	Blackburn	1 - 2	10	WLLWDLW--LWL	13	15	3	►	2	0	1	3-2 (1x)	31	5
	26th Dec	Man City	0 - 0	7	LWDW----W-DD	10	7	3	►	2	1	0	3-1 (1x)	37	8

Home fixture

Date	Opposition	03-04 scoreline	Played	Premiership history	Goals for	Goals against	No. of times Everton scored first	►	W	D	L	Most common score (no. times)	Avg time of first goal (mins)	Avg no. of corners	Home fixture
28th Dec	Charlton	2 - 2	5	------W-LWLD	7	7	1	►	1	0	0	1-2 (2x)	51	6	
1st Jan	Tottenham	0 - 3	12	LLLDDDLLLDLL	14	26	6	►	0	1	5	3-2 (3x)	25	4	
3rd Jan	Portsmouth	1 - 0	1	----------W	1	0	1	►	1	0	0	1-0 (1x)	78	6	👕
15th Jan	Middlesbro	0 - 1	9	W--WL-DLWLDL	12	13	4	►	2	1	1	1-2 (2x)	30	5	
22nd Jan	Charlton	0 - 1	5	------W-WLWL	8	5	3	►	3	0	0	4-1 (1x)	36	6	👕
2nd Feb	Norwich	n/a	3	LLW--------	3	7	2	►	1	0	1	2-1 (1x)	28	4	
5th Feb	Southampton	3 - 3	12	DWLDDLLLLWLD	11	17	4	►	2	2	0	2-0 (3x)	35	7	
12th Feb	Chelsea	0 - 1	12	LWDDLWDDWDLL	16	16	2	►	1	1	0	1-1 (2x)	37	6	
26th Feb	Aston Villa	0 - 0	12	LDDLLLLLLDLD	6	19	2	►	0	0	2	0-0 (4x)	24	4	
5th Mar	Blackburn	0 - 1	10	WLLWLWD--LWL	8	12	2	►	2	0	0	2-1 (2x)	38	6	
19th Mar	Liverpool	0 - 0	12	LLDWDDLWLDDD	10	13	6	►	2	2	2	1-1 (3x)	36	4	
2nd Apr	West Brom	n/a	1	----------W-	2	1	0	►	0	0	0	1-2 (1x)	23	10	
9th Apr	C Palace	n/a	3	L-W--L------	4	5	1	►	1	0	0	3-1 (1x)	44	10	👕
16th Apr	Arsenal	1 - 2	12	LLDWLLLLLLLL	11	30	1	►	0	0	1	4-1 (2x)	44	4	
20th Apr	Man Utd	3 - 4	12	LLWLLLLDLLLL	10	26	2	►	1	0	1	0-2 (4x)	45	6	👕
23rd Apr	Birmingham	1 - 0	2	---------DW	2	1	1	►	1	0	0	1-1 (1x)	80	7	👕
30th Apr	Fulham	1 - 2	3	---------LLL	1	6	0	►	0	0	0	2-0 (2x)	81	8	
7th May	Newcastle	2 - 2	11	-LWLWDWLDLWD	12	14	4	►	4	0	0	2-0 (2x)	46	6	👕
14th May	Bolton	0 - 2	5	---D-D---DWL	5	6	1	►	1	0	0	2-2 (1x)	54	6	

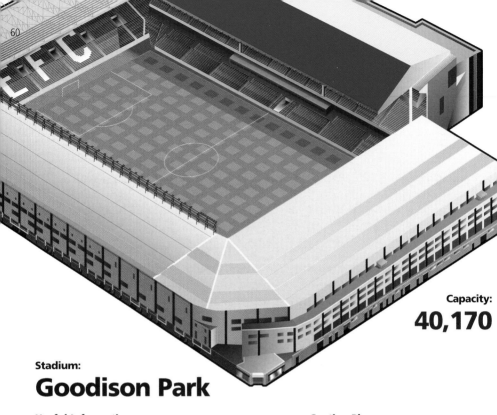

Capacity:
40,170

Stadium:
Goodison Park

Useful Information
Website: **www.evertonfc.com**
Address: **Goodison Park,
Liverpool L4 4EL**
Main Switchboard: **0151 330 2200**

Travel Information
Car Parking: 1000 spaces are available at Stanley Park, costing £6. Street parking is residents only.
By Train: Take any train from Liverpool Central which is heading for Ormskirk or Kirkby and alight at Kirkdale, a 10 minute walk from the ground.
By Bus: The number 19 runs from the Queen's Square bus station to Walton Lane; the number 20 runs along Spellow Lane.

Seating Plan

Top Balcony
Main Stand
Family Enclosure
Park Stand
Family Area
Away Fans
Disabled Fans
Gwladys Street Stand (Lower Tier)
Gwladys Street Stand (Upper Tier)
Bullens Road Stand (Paddock)
Bullens Road Stand (Lower Tier)
Bullens Road Stand (Upper Tier)

Area Map

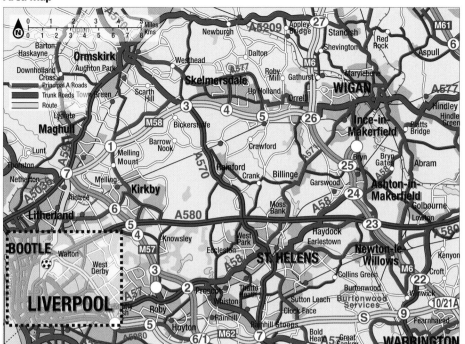

Local Map

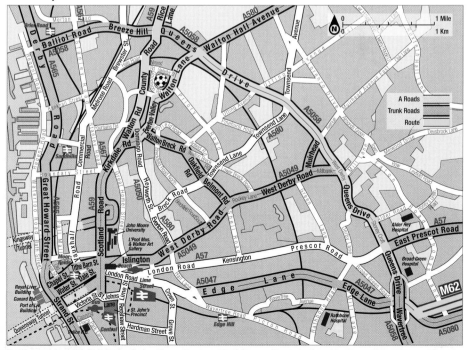

Fulham

Manager: **Chris Coleman**

Club Honours and Records
Division 1: 2000-01
Division 2: 1948-49, 1998-99
Division 3 (South): 1931-32

Squad List (stats from 2003-04 season)

Position		Appearances	Apps as Sub	Goals/Clean Sheets	Assists	Yellow Cards	Red Cards
G	M.Crossley	1					
G	E.van der Sar	37		15			
D	C.Bocanegra	15				2	1
D	J.Bonnissel	16			1		
D	A.Goma	23				5	
D	A.Green	4				1	
D	J.Harley	3	1				
D	Z.Knight	30	1		1	4	
D	D.Leacock	3	1			2	
D	A.Melville	9					
D	I.Pearce	12	1		1		
D	M.Volz	32	1			5	
M	L.Boa Morte	32	1	9	8	9	1
M	M.Buari	1	2				
M	L.Clark	25		2	4	2	
M	S.Davis	22	2	5	4	5	
M	M.Djetou	19	7			3	
M	J.Inamoto	15	7	2	1	8	
M	S.Legwinski	30	2		2	7	1
M	S.Malbranque	38		6	16	3	
M	M.Pembridge	9	3	1		1	
M	B.Petta	3	6				
M	Z.Rehman		1				
F	B.Hayles	10	16	4	3	2	
F	C.John	3	5	4	1	1	
F	S.Marlet	1	1				
F	B.McBride	5	11	4	1		
F	D.Pratley		1				
F	L.Saha	20	1	13	5	1	
F	F.Sava		6	1			

Five Season Form

Games Won	Games Drawn	Games Lost	Goals For	Goals Against	Goal Difference
41%	**29%**	**30%**	**196**	**213**	**-17**

Ten Season Form

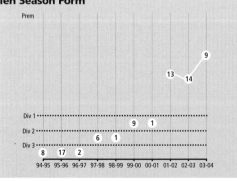

E.van der Sar
M.Crossley

J.Bonnissel
C.Bocanegra

A.Goma
I.Pearce
A.Melville

Z.Knight
I.Pearce

L.Clark
S.Legwinski
M.Pembridge

M.Volz
D.Leacock
M.Djetou

L.Boa Morte
S.Malbranque

S.Legwinski
M.Djetou
J.Inamoto

S.Davis
S.Legwinski

L.Saha
B.Hayles
B.McBride
C.John

S.Malbranque
J.Inamoto

Top Goalscorer
Louis Saha

13 Goals

	Left Foot	Right Foot	Header
Total	**8**	**4**	**1**
% of team's goals **25%**			

Goal Breakdown
(stats from 2003-04 season)

	Set Piece	Open Play	Total
Louis Saha	2	11	**13**
Luis Boa Morte	2	7	**9**
Steed Malbranque	2	4	**6**
Sean Davis	1	4	**5**
Barry Hayles	2	2	**4**
Brian McBride	1	3	**4**
Collins John	2	2	**4**
Lee Clark	–	2	**2**
Junichi Inamoto		2	**2**
Mark Pembridge	1	–	**1**
Steve Marlet	–	1	**1**
Facundo Sava	–	1	**1**

Premiership Statistics

First Goal Scored (average)

Home	Away
30 mins	**37** mins

First Goal Conceded (average)

Home	Away
19 mins	**16** mins

Clean Sheets	Failed To Score
15	**9** matches

Corners Per Game (average)	Average shots on target
4	**5**

Most Common Result:
2-0 (eight times)

Most First Goals:
6 - Louis Saha

Hat-Tricks:
None

Fastest Goal (mins):
1 - Luis Boa Morte v A Villa (H)
1 - Louis Saha v Birmingham (A)

Fastest Booking (mins):
8 - Alain Goma v Birmingham (A)

Highest Attendance:
18,306 v Man Utd 28/02/04

Lowest Attendance:
13,981 v Blackburn 12/04/04

Average Attendance: 16,342

Season Progression

7 7 5 4 5 7 8 9 7 9

Pos			W	D	L	Pts
9 Fulham			14	10	14	52

AUG SEPT OCT NOV DEC JAN FEB MAR APR MAY

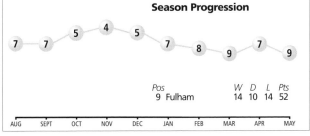

Fulham

Enhanced Fixture List 2004-05

In this fixture...

Date	Opposition	03-04 scoreline	Played	Premiership history	Goals for	Goals against	No. of times ⚽	►	W	D	L	Most common score (no. times)	Avg time of first goal (mins)	Avg no corr
14th Aug	Man City	0 - 0	2	----------LD	1	4	1	►	0	0	1	4-1 (1x)	2	2
21st Aug	Bolton	2 - 1	3	---------WWW	9	2	1	►	1	0	0	4-1 (1x)	43	5
25th Aug	Middlesbro	3 - 2	3	---------WWW	6	3	1	►	1	0	0	3-2 (1x)	32	7
30th Aug	Portsmouth	1 - 1	1	-----------D	1	1	0	►	0	0	0	1-1 (1x)	85	3
11th Sep	Arsenal	0 - 1	3	---------LLL	1	5	0	►	0	0	0	0-1 (2x)	48	6
18th Sep	West Brom	n/a	1	---------L-	0	1	0	►	0	0	0	1-0 (1x)	N/A	7
25th Sep	Southampton	2 - 0	3	---------WDW	6	3	3	►	2	1	0	2-2 (1x)	29	7
4th Oct	C Palace	n/a	These teams have never played each other in the Premiership											
16th Oct	Liverpool	1 - 2	3	---------LWL	4	6	1	►	1	0	0	3-2 (1x)	23	5
23rd Oct	Aston Villa	0 - 3	3	---------LLL	1	8	0	►	0	0	0	3-1 (1x)	51	4
30th Oct	Tottenham	2 - 1	3	---------LWW	5	5	0	►	0	0	0	3-2 (1x)	57	8
6th Nov	Newcastle	1 - 3	3	---------DLL	2	6	0	►	0	0	0	3-1 (1x)	75	4
13th Nov	Chelsea	0 - 1	3	---------DDL	1	2	0	►	0	0	0	1-1 (1x)	55	4
20th Nov	Everton	1 - 3	3	---------LLL	2	7	0	►	0	0	0	3-1 (1x)	61	8
27th Nov	Blackburn	3 - 4	3	---------WLL	5	8	1	►	1	0	0	3-4 (1x)	29	4
4th Dec	Norwich	n/a	These teams have never played each other in the Premiership											
13th Dec	Man Utd	1 - 1	3	---------LDD	4	5	1	►	0	1	0	1-1 (2x)	48	4
20th Dec	Charlton	1 - 3	3	---------DWL	3	4	1	►	1	0	0	3-1 (1x)	53	5
26th Dec	Arsenal	0 - 0	3	---------LLD	2	6	0	►	0	0	0	4-1 (1x)	20	3

Home fixture

Date	Opposition	03-04 scoreline	Played	Premiership history	Goals for	Goals against	No. of times Fulham scored first and the result that followed					Most common score (no. times)	Avg time of first goal (mins)	Avg no. of corners	
							⚽	▶	W	D	L				
28th Dec	Birmingham	0 - 0	2	----------LD	0	1	0	▶	0	0	0	0-1 (1x)	N/A	4	
1st Jan	C Palace	n/a		These teams have never played each other in the Premiership											
3rd Jan	Southampton	0 - 0	3	---------DLD	3	5	2	▶	0	1	1	4-2 (1x)	11	5	
15th Jan	West Brom	n/a	1	----------W-	3	0	1	▶	1	0	0	3-0 (1x)	72	2	
22nd Jan	Birmingham	2 - 2	2	----------DD	2	2	1	▶	0	1	0	2-2 (1x)	1	2	
2nd Feb	Aston Villa	1 - 2	3	---------DWL	3	3	1	▶	0	0	1	2-1 (1x)	8	7	
5th Feb	Liverpool	0 - 0	3	---------DLD	0	2	0	▶	0	0	0	0-0 (2x)	N/A	5	
12th Feb	Newcastle	2 - 3	3	---------WWL	7	5	2	▶	1	0	1	3-1 (1x)	31	4	
26th Feb	Tottenham	3 - 0	3	---------LDW	4	5	2	▶	1	1	0	4-0 (1x)	19	5	
5th Mar	Charlton	2 - 0	3	---------DWW	3	0	2	▶	2	0	0	2-0 (1x)	27	4	
19th Mar	Man Utd	3 - 1	3	---------LLW	5	7	2	▶	1	0	1	3-2 (1x)	4	4	
2nd Apr	Portsmouth	2 - 0	1	----------W	2	0	1	▶	1	0	0	2-0 (1x)	30	2	
9th Apr	Bolton	2 - 0	3	---------DDW	2	0	1	▶	1	0	0	0-0 (2x)	45	3	
16th Apr	Man City	2 - 2	2	----------LD	2	3	0	▶	0	0	0	2-2 (1x)	73	3	
19th Apr	Middlesbro	1 - 2	3	---------LDL	4	6	0	▶	0	0	0	2-1 (2x)	79	8	
23rd Apr	Chelsea	1 - 2	3	---------LDL	4	6	0	▶	0	0	0	3-2 (1x)	35	3	
30th Apr	Everton	2 - 1	3	---------WWW	6	1	3	▶	3	0	0	2-0 (2x)	38	6	
7th May	Blackburn	2 - 0	3	---------LLW	3	5	1	▶	1	0	0	3-0 (1x)	33	5	
14th May	Norwich	n/a		These teams have never played each other in the Premiership											

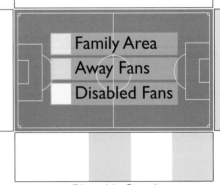

Stadium:

Craven Cottage

Capacity:

19,148

Useful Information

Website: www.fulhamfc.com
Address: **Craven Cottage, Stevenage Road, Fulham, London SW6 6HH**
Main Switchboard: **0870 442 1222**

Travel Information

Car Parking: There is very limited car parking on matchdays, so public transport is recommended for visiting supporters.

By Tube: Craven Cottage is a 10 minute walk from Putney Bridge station, which is on the Wimbledon branch of the District Line.

By Bus: Numbers 74 (to Roehampton) and 220 (to Wandsworth) both pass outside the ground.

Seating Plan

Stevenage Road Stand

Hammersmith End

Putney End

Family Area
Away Fans
Disabled Fans

Riverside Stand

Area Map

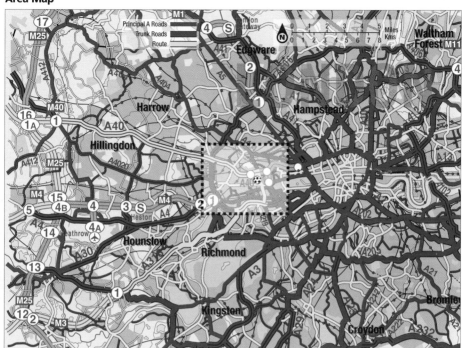

Local Map

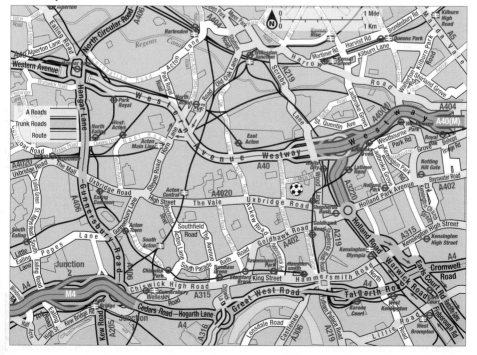

Liverpool

Manager: **Rafael Benitez**

Club Honours and Records

Football League: 1900-01, 1905-06, 1921-22, 1922-23, 1946-47, 1963-64, 1965-66, 1972-73, 1975-76, 1976-77, 1978-79, 1979-80, 1981-82, 1982-83, 1983-84, 1985-86, 1987-88, 1989-90
Division 2: 1893-94, 1895-96, 1904-05, 1961-62
FA Cup: 1965, 1974, 1986, 1989, 1992, 2001
League Cup: 1981, 1982, 1983, 1984, 1995, 2001
League Super Cup: 1986
European Cup: 1976-77, 1977-78, 1980-81, 1983-84
European Super Cup: 1977, 2001
UEFA Cup: 1972-73, 1975-76, 2000-01

Squad List (stats from 2003-04 season)

Position		Appearances	Apps as Sub	Goals/Clean Sheets	Assists	Yellow Cards	Red Cards
G	J.Dudek	30		13			
G	P.Jones	2		1			
G	C.Kirkland	6		1		1	
G	P.Luzi Bernardi		1				
D	J.Carragher	22			1	2	
D	S.Finnan	19	3		2	4	
D	S.Henchoz	15	3			3	
D	S.Hyypia	38		4		1	
D	J.Otsemobor	4				1	
D	J.Riise	22	6		4		
D	D.Traore	7					
M	I.Biscan	27	2			4	
M	B.Cheyrou	9	3	2			
M	S.Diao	2	1		1	1	
M	S.Gerrard	34		4	9	2	
M	D.Hamann	25		2	1	6	
M	D.Murphy	19	12	5	4	2	
M	V.Smicer	15	5	3	3	1	
M	J.Welsh		1			1	
F	M.Baros	6	7	1	3	2	
F	E.Diouf	20	6		5	9	1
F	E.Heskey	25	10	7	5	1	
F	H.Kewell	36		7	3	6	
F	A.Le Tallec	3	10		1		
F	M.Owen	29		16	5		
F	F.Sinama-Pongolle	3	12	2	3		

Five Season Form

Games Won	Games Drawn	Games Lost	Goals For	Goals Against	Goal Difference
51%	**26%**	**23%**	**220**	**177**	**+43**

Ten Season Form

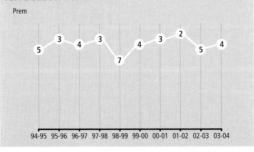

Prem

5 — 3 — 4 — 3 — 7 — 4 — 3 — 2 — 5 — 4

94-95 95-96 96-97 97-98 98-99 99-00 00-01 01-02 02-03 03-04

Formation and Line-ups:

J.Dudek
C.Kirkland
P.Jones

J.Riise
J.Carragher
D.Traore

S.Hyypia

I.Biscan
S.Henchoz

J.Carragher
S.Finnan
J.Otsemobor

H.Kewell
V.Smicer

D.Hamann
V.Smicer
D.Murphy

S.Gerrard
D.Murphy

D.Murphy
E.Diouf

E.Heskey
H.Kewell
M.Baros

M.Owen
E.Heskey
F.Sinama-Pongolle

Top Goalscorer
Michael Owen

16 Goals

	Left Foot	Right Foot	Header
Total	3	12	1

% of team's goals **29%**

Goal Breakdown
(stats from 2003-04 season)

	Set Piece	Open Play	Total
Michael Owen	6	10	**16**
Emile Heskey	-	7	**7**
Harry Kewell	-	7	**7**
Danny Murphy	4	1	**5**
Steven Gerrard	1	3	**4**
Sami Hyypia	4	-	**4**
Vladimir Smicer	2	1	**3**
Dietmar Hamann	1	1	**2**
Bruno Cheyrou	-	2	**2**
F Sinama-Pongolle	1	1	**2**
Milan Baros	-	1	**1**

Premiership Statistics

First Goal Scored (average)

Home	Away
33 mins	**25** mins

First Goal Conceded (average)

Home	Away
27 mins	**22** mins

Clean Sheets	Failed To Score
15	**9** matches

Corners Per Game (average)	Average shots on target
7	**6**

Most Common Result:
0-0 (six times)

Most First Goals:
9 - Michael Owen

Hat-Tricks:
None

Fastest Goal (mins):
3 - Michael Owen v Man City (H)

Fastest Booking (mins):
7 - Steven Gerrard v Middlesbrough (H)

Highest Attendance:
44,374 v Arsenal 04/10/03

Lowest Attendance:
34,663 v Portsmouth 17/03/04

Average Attendance: 42,677

Season Progression

9 8 9 6 6 5 6 4 4 4

Pos
4 Liverpool

W	D	L	Pts
16	12	10	60

AUG SEPT OCT NOV DEC JAN FEB MAR APR MAY

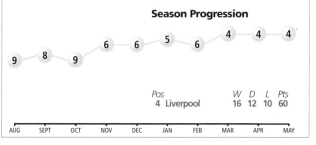

Liverpool

Enhanced Fixture List 2004-05

In this fixture...

Date	Opposition	03-04 scoreline	Played	Premiership history	Goals for	Goals against	No. of times Liverpool scored first		W	D	L	Most common score (no. times)	Avg time of first goal (mins)	Avg no score
14th Aug	Tottenham	1 - 2	12	LDDWWDLLLLWL	17	19	3	►	2	0	1	2-1 (3x)	40	5
21st Aug	Man City	2 - 1	7	DWWW----W-LW	17	7	5	►	4	0	1	2-1 (2x)	29	8
25th Aug	Portsmouth	3 - 0	1	----------W	3	0	1	►	1	0	0	3-0 (1x)	6	10
29th Aug	Bolton	2 - 2	5	---W-D---LWD	8	7	3	►	2	1	0	2-3 (1x)	45	5
11th Sep	West Brom	n/a	1	----------W-	2	0	1	►	1	0	0	2-0 (1x)	56	7
20th Sep	Man Utd	1 - 0	12	DLLDLDLDWWLW	9	16	5	►	3	2	0	0-1 (3x)	44	4
25th Sep	Norwich	n/a	3	WLW---------	8	2	1	►	1	0	0	4-1 (1x)	15	10
3rd Oct	Chelsea	1 - 0	12	DLDDLLLLLLLW	6	21	2	►	1	0	1	2-1 (2x)	40	6
16th Oct	Fulham	2 - 1	3	---------WLW	6	4	2	►	2	0	0	3-2 (1x)	31	6
23rd Oct	Charlton	0 - 1	5	------D-WWWL	10	5	2	►	2	0	0	3-3 (1x)	37	6
30th Oct	Blackburn	3 - 1	10	LLLWLDW--DDW	16	20	5	►	2	2	1	1-3 (2x)	34	6
6th Nov	Birmingham	3 - 1	2	----------DW	5	3	1	►	0	1	0	3-1 (1x)	30	4
13th Nov	C Palace	n/a	3	W-D--W------	7	1	2	►	2	0	0	5-0 (1x)	18	7
20th Nov	Middlesbro	0 - 0	9	W--LD-WLLWLD	11	11	4	►	3	1	0	1-0 (3x)	26	6
28th Nov	Arsenal	1 - 2	12	LDWWWWDWWLDL	22	9	6	►	5	0	1	4-0 (2x)	34	7
4th Dec	Aston Villa	0 - 0	12	LLLWLLWDWWWD	16	14	8	►	5	0	3	2-1 (2x)	26	5
11th Dec	Everton	3 - 0	12	LLLDDLDDWWWW	14	14	5	►	3	1	1	2-0 (3x)	37	5
18th Dec	Newcastle	1 - 1	11	-LWWWWWWWDD	26	14	8	►	7	1	0	4-3 (2x)	40	7
26th Dec	West Brom	n/a	1	----------W-	6	0	1	►	1	0	0	0-6 (1x)	15	6

Home fixture

Date	Opposition	03-04 scoreline	Played	Premiership history	Goals for	Goals against	No. of times Liverpool scored first and the result that followed ⚽		► W	D	L	Most common score (no. times)	Avg time of first goal (mins)	Avg no. of corners	Home
28th Dec	Southampton	1 - 2	12	DWWDWLWDWDWL	27	14	6	►	5	1	0	1-1 (3x)	32	8	🎽
1st Jan	Chelsea	1 - 2	12	WWWWWWDWDWWL	25	11	9	►	8	1	0	1-0 (3x)	44	6	🎽
3rd Jan	Norwich	n/a	3	LDW--------	4	4	1	►	1	0	0	2-2 (1x)	30	4	
15th Jan	Man Utd	1 - 2	12	LDWWLLDLWWLL	21	21	4	►	4	0	0	2-0 (3x)	43	5	🎽
22nd Jan	Southampton	0 - 2	12	LLWWWDWDDLWL	17	17	5	►	3	2	0	2-0 (2x)	44	5	
1st Feb	Charlton	2 - 3	5	------L-WWLL	8	6	3	►	2	0	1	3-2 (1x)	28	5	
5th Feb	Fulham	0 - 0	3	---------DWD	2	0	1	►	1	0	0	0-0 (2x)	36	8	🎽
12th Feb	Birmingham	3 - 0	2	----------LW	4	2	1	►	1	0	0	2-1 (1x)	53	6	
26th Feb	Blackburn	4 - 0	10	WLWWDDW--WDW	18	7	6	►	5	1	0	2-1 (2x)	33	6	🎽
5th Mar	Newcastle	1 - 1	11	-LDLDWWDLWLD	15	15	3	►	2	1	0	1-1 (3x)	32	4	
19th Mar	Everton	0 - 0	12	WWDLDDWLWDDD	13	10	3	►	2	1	0	1-1 (3x)	50	8	🎽
2nd Apr	Bolton	3 - 1	5	---W-W---DWW	13	5	4	►	3	1	0	5-2 (1x)	39	9	🎽
9th Apr	Man City	2 - 2	7	DDLD----D-WD	11	9	3	►	1	2	0	1-1 (3x)	42	6	
16th Apr	Tottenham	0 - 0	12	WLDDWWWWWWWD	25	10	8	►	6	1	1	2-1 (2x)	36	7	🎽
19th Apr	Portsmouth	0 - 1	1	-----------L	0	1	0	►	0	0	0	1-0 (1x)	N/A	3	
23rd Apr	C Palace	n/a	3	D-W--W------	10	2	3	►	2	1	0	1-6 (1x)	33	7	
30th Apr	Middlesbro	2 - 0	9	W--WW-WDDWDW	18	4	6	►	6	0	0	2-0 (2x)	34	8	🎽
7th May	Arsenal	2 - 4	12	WLWDWWDWLDDL	10	10	7	►	5	1	1	0-1 (4x)	52	4	
14th May	Aston Villa	1 - 0	12	LWWWWWLDWLDW	21	11	9	►	7	1	1	3-0 (3x)	34	6	🎽

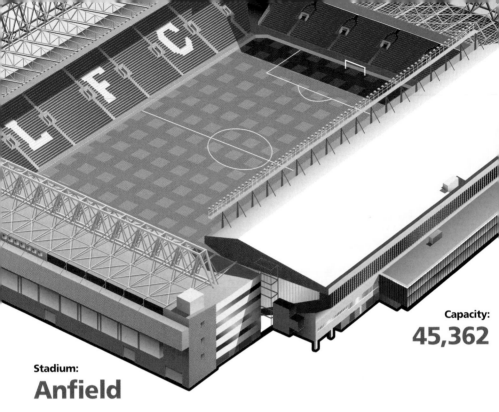

Capacity:
45,362

Stadium:
Anfield

Useful Information
Website: **www.liverpoolfc.tv**
Address: **Anfield Road, Liverpool L4 0TH**
Main Switchboard: **0151 263 2361**

Travel Information
By Train: Lime Street Railway Station is in the town centre, 2 miles from Anfield. Kirkdale Railway Station is 30 minutes walk from the ground.
By Bus: Numbers 26 and 27 run from Paradise Street bus station. Numbers 5, 17b, 17c, 17d and 217 run from Queen Square bus station. There is a 'Soccerbus' service that runs from Sandhills station to Anfield for two hours before the match and 50 minutes afterwards.

Seating Plan

Centenary Stand (Upper Tier)

Executive Boxes

Centenary Stand (Lower Tier)

Anfield Road Stand (Upper Tier)

Anfield Road Stand (LowerTier)

Family Area

Away Fans

Disabled Fans

Kop Grandstand

Paddock Enclosure

Main Stand

Area Map

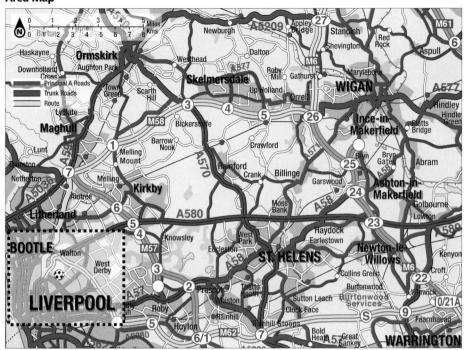

Local Map

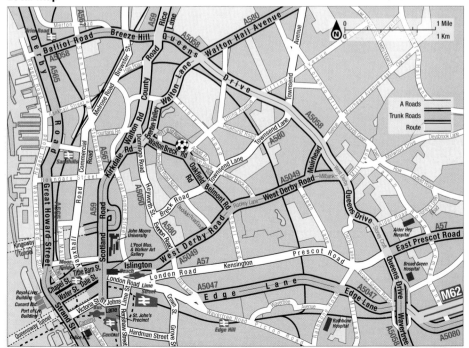

Manchester City
Manager: **Kevin Keegan**

Club Honours and Records
Football League: 1936-37, 1967-68
Division 1: 2001-02
Division 2: 1898-99, 1902-03, 1909-10, 1927-28, 1946-47, 1965-66
FA Cup: 1904, 1934, 1956, 1969
League Cup: 1970, 1976
Cup-Winners Cup: 1969-70

Five Season Form

Games Won	Games Drawn	Games Lost	Goals For	Goals Against	Goal Difference
43%	23%	34%	263	265	-2

Ten Season Form

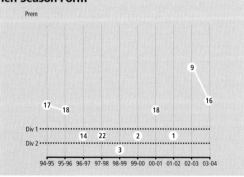

Squad List (stats from 2003-04 season)

Position		Appearances	Apps as Sub	Goals/Clean Sheets	Assists	Yellow Cards	Red Cards
G	D.James	17		3	1		
G	D.Seaman	19		4			
G	K.Stuhr-Ellegaard	2	2				
D	S.Distin	38		2		6	
D	R.Dunne	28	1			5	
D	S.Jihai	29	4	1	4	7	
D	S.Jordan		2				
D	D.Sommeil	18		1	1	3	
D	M.Tarnat	32		3	5	6	
D	D.Van Buyten	5					1
M	J.Barton	24	4	1	2	8	
M	E.Berkovic	1	3				
M	P.Bosvelt	22	3		3	3	
M	S.McManaman	20	2		5	1	
M	C.Reyna	19	4	1	2		
M	A.Sibierski	18	15	5	5	1	
M	T.Sinclair	20	9	1	2	2	
M	D.Tiatto	1	4		1	1	
M	S.Wright-Phillips	32	2	7	3	2	1
F	N.Anelka	31	1	16	9	1	1
F	S.Elliott		2				
F	R.Fowler	23	8	7	1	2	
F	J.Macken	7	8	1	2		
F	P.Wanchope	12	10	6	5	1	

Formation and Line-ups

Field positions:

- **D.Seaman**
  D.James
  K.Stuhr-Ellegaard
- **M.Tarnat**
  S.Distin
- **S.Distin**
  D.Van Buyten
  D.Sommeil
- **R.Dunne**
  D.Sommeil
- **S.Jihai**
  S.Wright-Phillips
  D.Sommeil
- **T.Sinclair**
  S.McManaman
  A.Sibierski
- **J.Barton**
  P.Bosvelt
  S.McManaman
- **C.Reyna**
  S.McManaman
- **S.Wright-Phillips**
  T.Sinclair
- **R.Fowler**
  P.Wanchope
- **N.Anelka**
  J.Macken

Top Goalscorer
Nicolas Anelka

16 Goals

	Left Foot	Right Foot	Header
Total	**3**	**12**	**1**

% of team's goals **29%**

Goal Breakdown
(stats from 2003-04 season)

	Set Piece	Open Play	Total
Nicolas Anelka	5	11	**16**
Robbie Fowler	1	6	**7**
S Wright-Phillips	1	6	**7**
Paulo Wanchope	-	6	**6**
Antoine Sibierski	1	4	**5**
Michael Tarnat	3	-	**3**
Sylvain Distin	1	1	**2**
Trevor Sinclair	-	1	**1**
Sun Jihai	-	1	**1**
Jonathan Macken	-	1	**1**
Claudio Reyna	-	1	**1**
David Sommeil	1	-	**1**
Joey Barton	-	1	**1**

Premiership Statistics

First Goal Scored (average)

Home	Away
29 mins	**29** mins

First Goal Conceded (average)

Home	Away
33 mins	**33** mins

Clean Sheets	Failed To Score
7	**10** matches

Corners Per Game (average)	Average shots on target
6	**6**

Most Common Result:
1-1 (seven times)

Most First Goals:
10 - Nicolas Anelka

Hat-Tricks:
Nicolas Anelka v Aston Villa (H)

Fastest Goal (mins):
3 - Robbie Fowler v Man Utd (H)

Fastest Booking (mins):
9 - Richard Dunne v Bolton (A)

Highest Attendance:
47,304 v Chelsea 28/02/04

Lowest Attendance:
44,307 v Charlton 07/01/04

Average Attendance: 46,834

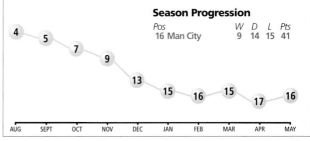

Season Progression

Pos	W	D	L	Pts
16 Man City	9	14	15	41

Positions by month: AUG 4, SEPT 5, OCT 7, NOV 9, DEC 13, JAN 15, FEB 16, MAR 15, APR 17, MAY 16

Manchester City

Enhanced Fixture List 2004-05

In this fixture...

	Date	Opposition	03-04 scoreline	Played	Premiership history	Goals for	Goals against	⚽ No. of times Man City scored first	►	W	D	L	Most common score (no. times)	Avg time of first goal (mins)	Avg no. of corner
	14th Aug	Fulham	0 - 0	2	----------WD	4	1	0	►	0	0	0	4-1 (1x)	21	6
	21st Aug	Liverpool	1 - 2	7	DLLL----L-WL	7	17	2	►	0	1	1	2-1 (2x)	47	4
	24th Aug	Birmingham	1 - 2	2	----------WL	3	2	2	►	1	0	1	2-1 (1x)	19	2
	28th Aug	Charlton	1 - 1	3	--------L-LD	2	6	1	►	0	1	0	1-4 (1x)	65	5
	11th Sep	Everton	5 - 1	7	LWWL----W-WW	20	9	5	►	5	0	0	5-1 (1x)	25	7
	18th Sep	C Palace	n/a	2	D-L---------	1	2	0	►	0	0	0	2-1 (1x)	58	7
	25th Sep	Arsenal	1 - 2	7	LDLL----L-LL	3	15	1	►	0	0	1	1-2 (2x)	59	5
	2nd Oct	Southampton	2 - 0	7	WWDD----W-LW	9	5	4	►	4	0	0	0-2 (2x)	48	4
	16th Oct	Chelsea	0 - 1	7	LDLL----L-LL	4	12	1	►	0	0	1	0-1 (3x)	22	7
	23rd Oct	Newcastle	0 - 3	6	-LDL----W-LL	2	10	1	►	1	0	0	2-0 (2x)	71	3
	1st Nov	Norwich	n/a	3	WDW---------	6	2	2	►	2	0	0	3-1 (1x)	48	9
	7th Nov	Man Utd	1 - 3	7	LLLL----D-DL	4	15	0	►	0	0	0	1-1 (2x)	64	4
	13th Nov	Blackburn	1 - 1	6	WLLD------DD	8	11	1	►	0	1	0	1-1 (2x)	54	9
	20th Nov	Portsmouth	2 - 4	1	----------L	2	4	0	►	0	0	0	4-2 (1x)	21	7
	27th Nov	Aston Villa	4 - 1	7	DWDW----L-WW	15	8	5	►	3	1	1	4-1 (1x)	39	6
	6th Dec	Middlesbro	1 - 2	5	L--L----D-LL	4	12	2	►	0	1	1	4-1 (1x)	36	5
	11th Dec	Tottenham	0 - 0	7	LLWD----L-LD	8	10	2	►	1	0	1	0-1 (2x)	32	6
	18th Dec	Bolton	3 - 1	3	---D------LW	4	4	1	►	0	1	0	2-0 (1x)	15	8
	26th Dec	Everton	0 - 0	7	WLDL----L-DD	7	10	3	►	1	1	1	3-1 (1x)	20	4

Home fixture

Date	Opposition	03-04 scoreline	Played	Premiership history	Goals for	Goals against	⚽	►	W	D	L	Most common score (no. times)	Avg time of first goal (mins)	Avg no. of corners	
28th Dec	West Brom	n/a	1	----------L-	1	2	0	►	0	0	0	1-2 (1x)	22	6	🎽
1st Jan	Southampton	1 - 3	7	WDDW----L-LL	8	10	2	►	2	0	0	0-1 (2x)	53	6	🎽
3rd Jan	Arsenal	1 - 2	7	LDLL----L-LL	3	16	0	►	0	0	0	2-1 (2x)	57	3	
15th Jan	C Palace	n/a	2	D-D---------	1	1	1	►	0	1	0	1-1 (1x)	18	7	🎽
22nd Jan	West Brom	n/a	1	----------W-	2	1	1	►	1	0	0	1-2 (1x)	51	3	
1st Feb	Newcastle	1 - 0	6	-WDD----L-WW	7	5	3	►	2	1	0	1-0 (2x)	36	7	🎽
5th Feb	Chelsea	0 - 1	7	WDLD----L-LL	6	14	1	►	1	0	0	5-0 (1x)	50	6	
12th Feb	Man Utd	4 - 1	7	DLLL----L-WW	12	13	4	►	2	1	1	2-3 (2x)	25	7	🎽
26th Feb	Norwich	n/a	3	LDD---------	3	4	0	►	0	0	0	1-1 (2x)	64	6	
5th Mar	Bolton	6 - 2	3	---W------WW	9	2	2	►	2	0	0	6-2 (1x)	21	7	🎽
19th Mar	Tottenham	1 - 1	7	LLLL----D-WD	5	8	3	►	1	1	1	1-0 (2x)	34	5	
2nd Apr	Charlton	3 - 0	3	--------L-DW	5	6	1	►	1	0	0	4-0 (1x)	43	5	
9th Apr	Liverpool	2 - 2	7	DDWD----D-LD	9	11	4	►	1	3	0	1-1 (3x)	41	7	🎽
16th Apr	Fulham	2 - 2	2	----------WD	3	2	2	►	1	1	0	2-2 (1x)	65	8	
20th Apr	Birmingham	0 - 0	2	----------WD	1	0	1	►	1	0	0	1-0 (1x)	72	10	🎽
23rd Apr	Blackburn	3 - 2	6	LLWL------LW	6	10	1	►	1	0	0	2-3 (2x)	18	4	
30th Apr	Portsmouth	1 - 1	1	----------D	1	1	0	►	0	0	0	1-1 (1x)	90	11	🎽
7th May	Aston Villa	1 - 1	7	LDDW----D-LD	6	8	3	►	1	1	1	1-1 (2x)	63	4	
14th May	Middlesbro	0 - 1	5	L--L----D-DL	1	4	0	►	0	0	0	0-1 (3x)	67	9	🎽

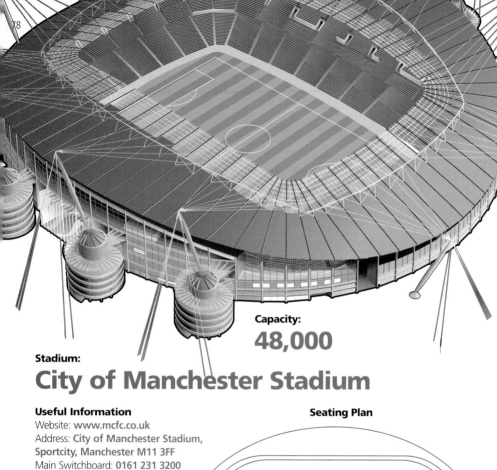

Capacity:

48,000

Stadium:

City of Manchester Stadium

Useful Information
Website: **www.mcfc.co.uk**
Address: **City of Manchester Stadium,
Sportcity, Manchester M11 3FF**
Main Switchboard: **0161 231 3200**

Travel Information
By Train: The nearest station
is Manchester Picadilly,
approx 1 mile from the stadium
By Bus: Numbers 216, 217,
and 230 to 237 run
from the city centre

Seating Plan

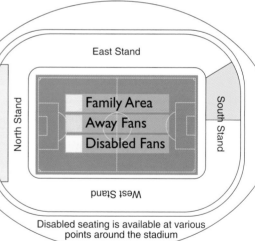

East Stand

North Stand

South Stand

Family Area
Away Fans
Disabled Fans

West Stand

Disabled seating is available at various
points around the stadium

Area Map

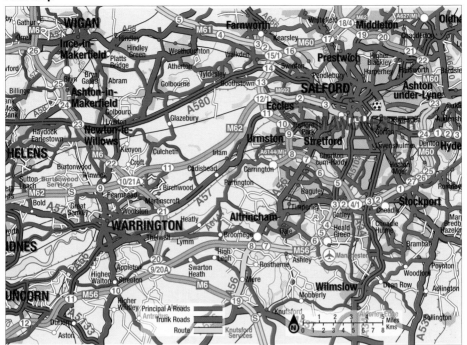

Local Map

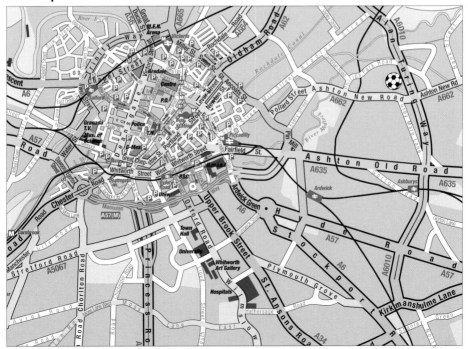

Manchester United

Manager: **Sir Alex Ferguson**

Club Honours and Records

Premier League: 1992-93, 1993-94, 1995-96, 1996-97, 1998-99, 1999-00, 2000-01, 2002-03
Football League: 1907-08, 1910-11, 1951-52, 1955-56, 1956-57, 1964-65, 1966-67
Division 2: 1935-36, 1974-75
FA Cup: 1909, 1948, 1963, 1977, 1983, 1985, 1990, 1994, 1996, 1999, 2004
League Cup: 1992
European Cup: 1967-68, 1998-99
European Super Cup: 1991
Cup-Winners Cup: 1990-91
Inter-continental Cup: 1999

Five Season Form

Games Won	Games Drawn	Games Lost	Goals For	Goals Against	Goal Difference
65%	18%	17%	248	190	+58

Ten Season Form

Prem

2 — 1 — 1 — 2 — 1 — 1 — 1 — 3 — 1 — 3

94-95 95-96 96-97 97-98 98-99 99-00 00-01 01-02 02-03 03-04

Squad List (stats from 2003-04 season)

Position		Appearances	Apps as Sub	Goals/Clean Sheets	Assists	Yellow Cards	Red Cards
G	R.Carroll	6		2			
G	T.Howard	32		12			
D	W.Brown	15	2		1	1	
D	R.Ferdinand	20			1		
D	G.Neville	30		2	4	5	
D	P.Neville	29	2		2	4	
D	J.O'Shea	32	1	2		1	
D	M.Silvestre	33	1		1	2	
M	N.Butt	12	9	1		2	
M	E.Djemba-Djemba	10	5		2	1	
M	D.Fletcher	17	5		2		2
M	Q.Fortune	18	5		3	2	
M	R.Giggs	29	4	7	12	3	
M	R.Keane	25	3	3	3	2	
M	Kleberson	10	2	2	3	1	
M	C.Ronaldo	15	14	4	6	3	1
M	P.Scholes	24	4	9	5	5	
F	D.Bellion	4	10	2	1		
F	D.Forlan	10	14	4	4	2	
F	L.Saha	9	3	7	3		
F	O.Solskjaer	7	6		2	2	
F	R.van Nistelrooy	31	1	20	4	4	

T.Howard
R.Carroll

J.O'Shea
Q.Fortune
P.Neville

M.Silvestre
J.O'Shea

R.Ferdinand
W.Brown
J.O'Shea

G.Neville
P.Neville
J.O'Shea

R.Giggs
C.Ronaldo
P.Scholes

P.Scholes
P.Neville
N.Butt

R.Keane
E.Djemba-Djemba
N.Butt

C.Ronaldo
D.Fletcher
O.Solskjaer
Kleberson

L.Saha
P.Scholes
R.Giggs

R.van Nistelrooy
D.Forlan

Top Goalscorer
Ruud van Nistelrooy

20 Goals

	Left Foot	Right Foot	Header
Total	1	16	3

% of team's goals 31%

Goal Breakdown
(stats from 2003-04 season)

	Set Piece	Open Play	Total
Ruud van Nistelrooy	5	15	20
Paul Scholes	-	9	9
Ryan Giggs	1	6	7
Louis Saha	2	5	7
Diego Forlan	-	4	4
Cristiano Ronaldo	2	2	4
Roy Keane	-	3	3
Gary Neville	-	2	2
John O'Shea	2	-	2
David Bellion	-	2	2
Kleberson	-	2	2
Nicky Butt	-	1	1

Premiership Statistics

First Goal Scored (average)

Home	Away
28 mins	**28** mins

First Goal Conceded (average)

Home	Away
18 mins	**44** mins

Clean Sheets	Failed To Score
14	**8** matches

Corners Per Game (average)	Average shots on target
5	**6**

Most Common Result:
0-1, 2-1 (six times)

Most First Goals:
7 - Ruud van Nistelrooy

Hat-Tricks:
Ruud van Nistelrooy v Leicester City (A)

Fastest Goal (mins):
4 - Cristiano Ronaldo v Aston Villa (A)

Fastest Booking (mins):
14 - Nicky Butt v Man City (A)
14 - Cristiano Ronaldo v Leeds (A)

Highest Attendance:
67,758 v Southampton 31/01/04
Lowest Attendance:
67,346 v Middlesbro 11/02/04
Average Attendance: 67,640

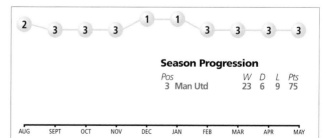

Season Progression

Pos		W	D	L	Pts
3	Man Utd	23	6	9	75

AUG   SEPT   OCT   NOV   DEC   JAN   FEB   MAR   APR   MAY

Manchester United

Enhanced Fixture List 2004-05

In this fixture...

Date	Opposition	03-04 scoreline	Played	Premiership history	Goals for	Goals against	⚽ No. of times Man Utd scored first	►	W	D	L	Most common score (no. times)	Avg time of first goal (mins)	Avg no. of corners
15th Aug	Chelsea	0 - 1	12	DLWWDWDLDWDL	16	15	4	►	4	0	0	1-1 (3x)	38	5
21st Aug	Norwich	n/a	3	WDW---------	4	2	3	►	2	1	0	1-0 (2x)	42	4
25th Aug	Everton	3 - 2	12	LWWWDWWWWWWW	28	10	9	►	9	0	0	2-0 (3x)	39	6
28th Aug	Blackburn	0 - 1	10	DLWWWWD--DLL	14	12	3	►	2	1	0	1-0 (2x)	40	6
11th Sep	Bolton	2 - 1	5	---W-D---WDW	13	2	3	►	3	0	0	1-2 (1x)	34	6
20th Sep	Liverpool	0 - 1	12	DWWDWDWDLLWL	16	9	7	►	5	2	0	0-1 (3x)	32	7
25th Sep	Tottenham	2 - 1	12	DWWLWWWDLLWWW	21	18	9	►	6	2	1	3-1 (2x)	39	6
2nd Oct	Middlesbro	2 - 3	9	W--WD-LWWLWL	16	11	4	►	4	0	0	2-3 (2x)	48	9
16th Oct	Birmingham	2 - 1	2	----------WW	3	1	1	►	1	0	0	1-2 (1x)	58	4
24th Oct	Arsenal	0 - 0	12	DWWWWLDDWLWD	16	5	6	►	6	0	0	1-0 (3x)	44	6
30th Oct	Portsmouth	0 - 1	1	----------L	0	1	0	►	0	0	0	1-0 (1x)	N/A	13
7th Nov	Man City	3 - 1	7	WWWW----D-DW	15	4	7	►	5	2	0	1-1 (2x)	26	6
14th Nov	Newcastle	2 - 1	11	-DDWLWWLDLWW	18	19	5	►	2	3	0	1-1 (3x)	39	3
20th Nov	Charlton	2 - 0	5	------W-WDWW	12	3	3	►	3	0	0	4-1 (2x)	31	9
27th Nov	West Brom	n/a	1	----------W-	3	1	0	►	0	0	0	1-3 (1x)	8	6
4th Dec	Southampton	3 - 2	12	WWWWWWWDWWWW	34	12	8	►	8	0	0	2-1 (5x)	35	8
13th Dec	Fulham	1 - 1	3	---------WDD	5	4	2	►	1	1	0	1-1 (2x)	27	2
18th Dec	C Palace	n/a	3	W-W--W-----	6	0	3	►	3	0	0	3-0 (1x)	38	7
26th Dec	Bolton	4 - 0	5	---W-D---LLW	9	4	3	►	2	0	1	4-0 (1x)	41	8

Home fixture

Date	Opposition	03-04 scoreline	Played	Premiership history	Goals for	Goals against	No. of times Man Utd scored first ⚽	►	W	D	L	Most common score (no. times)	Avg time of first goal (mins)	Avg no. of corners	Home
28th Dec	Aston Villa	2 - 0	12	LWWLDWDWWDWW	14	8	7	►	6	1	0	0-1 (3x)	53	5	
1st Jan	Middlesbro	1 - 0	9	D--WD-WWWWLW	16	9	7	►	5	2	0	0-1 (3x)	35	7	
3rd Jan	Tottenham	3 - 0	12	WWDWWWWWWWWW	26	4	10	►	10	0	0	2-0 (3x)	39	9	👕
15th Jan	Liverpool	2 - 1	12	WDLLWWDWLLWW	21	21	8	►	6	2	0	2-0 (3x)	35	4	
22nd Jan	Aston Villa	4 - 0	12	DWWDDWWWWWDW	19	4	8	►	8	0	0	1-0 (3x)	40	7	👕
1st Feb	Arsenal	1 - 1	12	WDDLWLLWLLDD	13	18	5	►	2	2	1	2-2 (2x)	34	4	
5th Feb	Birmingham	3 - 0	2	----------WW	5	0	2	►	2	0	0	3-0 (1x)	37	9	👕
12th Feb	Man City	1 - 4	7	DWWW----W-LL	13	12	3	►	3	0	0	2-3 (2x)	33	6	
26th Feb	Portsmouth	3 - 0	1	-----------W	3	0	1	►	1	0	0	3-0 (1x)	37	3	
5th Mar	C Palace	n/a	3	W-D--W------	6	1	3	►	2	1	0	1-1 (1x)	42	6	
19th Mar	Fulham	1 - 3	3	---------WWL	7	5	1	►	1	0	0	3-2 (1x)	42	8	👕
2nd Apr	Blackburn	2 - 1	10	WDWWDWW--WWW	22	9	7	►	7	0	0	3-1 (2x)	38	7	👕
9th Apr	Norwich	n/a	3	WWW---------	7	1	3	►	3	0	0	0-2 (2x)	13	4	
16th Apr	Chelsea	1 - 1	12	WLDDLDDWDLWD	17	17	3	►	2	1	0	1-1 (3x)	43	6	👕
20th Apr	Everton	4 - 3	12	WWLWWWWDWWWW	26	10	10	►	9	1	0	0-2 (4x)	30	5	
23rd Apr	Newcastle	0 - 0	11	-DWWDDDWWWWD	21	7	7	►	6	1	0	2-0 (3x)	22	6	👕
30th Apr	Charlton	2 - 0	5	------W-DWWW	11	4	3	►	3	0	0	0-2 (2x)	56	7	
7th May	West Brom	n/a	1	----------W-	1	0	1	►	1	0	0	1-0 (1x)	78	10	👕
14th May	Southampton	0 - 1	12	WWDLLLWWLWWL	22	18	5	►	5	0	0	1-3 (3x)	39	6	

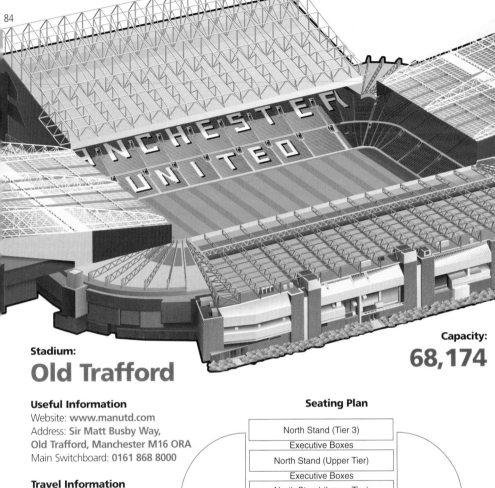

Stadium:
Old Trafford

Capacity:
68,174

Useful Information

Website: **www.manutd.com**
Address: **Sir Matt Busby Way,
Old Trafford, Manchester M16 ORA**
Main Switchboard: **0161 868 8000**

Travel Information

Car Parking: There is a
large official car park on
Elevator Road, and various
smaller car parks nearby.
By Train: (matchdays only):
Special services run from the
clubs own railway station
adjacent to the South Stand.
By Metrolink: Old Trafford
station is about 1/2 mile away
from the ground.
By Bus: Numbers 114, 230, 252
and 253 all run from the city centre
to the ground.

Seating Plan

North Stand (Tier 3)

Executive Boxes

North Stand (Upper Tier)

Executive Boxes

North Stand (Lower Tier)

West Stand (Upper Tier)

Executive Boxes

West Stand (Lower Tier)

Family Area

Away Fans

Disabled Fans

East Stand (Lower Tier)

Executive Boxes

East Stand (Upper Tier)

South Stand

Executive Boxes

Area Map

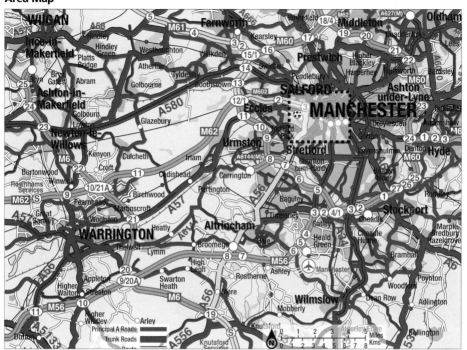

Local Map

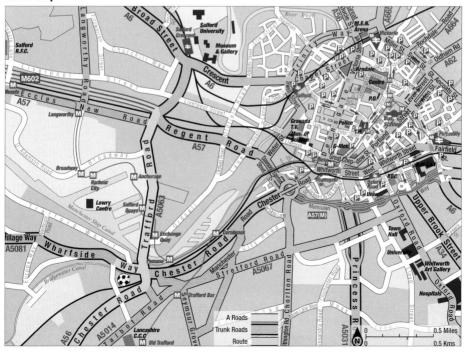

Middlesbrough

Manager: **Steve McClaren**

Club Honours and Records

Division 1: 1994-95
Division 2: 1926-27, 1928-29, 1973-74
League Cup: 2004
Amateur Cup: 1895, 1898
Anglo-Scottish Cup: 1976

Five Season Form

Games Won	Games Drawn	Games Lost	Goals For	Goals Against	Goal Difference
32%	28%	40%	218	239	-21

Ten Season Form

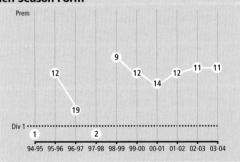

Squad List (stats from 2003-04 season)

Position		Appearances	Apps as Sub	Goals/Clean Sheets	Assists	Yellow Cards	Red Cards
G	B.Jones	1					
G	C.Nash	1		1			
G	M.Schwarzer	36		13			
D	C.Cooper	17	2			3	
D	A.Davies	8	2				
D	U.Ehiogu	16			1	3	
D	D.Mills	28			1	10	
D	S.Parnaby	8	5		1	1	
D	F.Queudrue	31			2	4	
D	C.Riggott	14	3			2	
D	G.Southgate	27		1	2	1	
D	R.Stockdale		2				
D	A.Wright	2					
M	G.Boateng	35			2	6	
M	Doriva	19	2		2	6	
M	S.Downing	7	13		1		
M	J.Greening	17	8	1		5	
M	Juninho	26	5	8	2	2	
M	C.Marinelli	1		1			
M	G.Mendieta	30	1	2	9	3	
M	B.Zenden	31		4	4	3	1
F	M.Christie	7	3	1	1	1	
F	J.Job	19	5	5	3	1	
F	M.Maccarone	13	10	6	4	3	
F	J.Morrison		1				
F	S.Nemeth	17	15	9	2	2	
F	M.Ricketts	7	16	2	2	2	

M.Schwarzer
C.Nash
B.Jones

F.Queudrue
S.Parnaby

G.Southgate
C.Cooper
C.Riggott

U.Ehiogu
C.Riggott
C.Cooper

B.Zenden
S.Downing
J.Greening

D.Mills
S.Parnaby
A.Davies

Juninho
Doriva
B.Zenden

G.Boateng
Doriva

G.Mendieta
J.Greening

J.Job
M.Maccarone
M.Ricketts
M.Christie

S.Nemeth
Juninho

Top Goalscorer
Szilard Nemeth

9 Goals

	Left Foot	Right Foot	Header
Total	2	7	-

% of team's goals **20%**

Goal Breakdown
(stats from 2003-04 season)

	Set Piece	Open Play	Total
Szilard Nemeth	2	7	9
Juninho	2	6	8
Massimo Maccarone	1	5	6
Joseph-Desire Job	1	4	5
Boudewijn Zenden	1	3	4
Michael Ricketts	2	-	2
Gaizka Mendieta	1	1	2
Gareth Southgate	1	-	1
Malcolm Christie	-	1	1
Jonathan Greening	-	1	1
Carlos Marinelli	-	1	1

Premiership Statistics
First Goal Scored (average)

Home	Away
19 mins	**27** mins

First Goal Conceded (average)

Home	Away
22 mins	**21** mins

Clean Sheets	Failed To Score
14	**14** matches

Corners Per Game (average)	Average shots on target
5	**5**

Most Common Result:
0-0 (six times)

Most First Goals:
4 - Szilard Nemeth, Juninho, Boudewijn Zenden

Hat-Tricks:
None

Fastest Goal (mins):
5 - Gaizka Mendieta v Birmingham (H)

Fastest Booking (mins):
3 - Ugo Ehiogu v Fulham (H)

Highest Attendance:
34,738 v Man Utd 28/12/03

Lowest Attendance:
26,721 v Charlton 13/12/03

Average Attendance: 30,397

Season Progression

Pos   W D L Pts
11 Middlesbrough   13 9 16 48

AUG 19, SEPT 12, OCT 17, NOV 10, DEC 15, JAN 12, FEB 13, MAR 11, APR 12, MAY 11

Middlesbrough

Enhanced Fixture List 2004-05

In this fixture...

	Date	Opposition	03-04 scoreline	Played	Premiership history	Goals for	Goals against	⚽ No of times Middlesbrough scored first	►	W	D	L	Most common score (no. times)	Avg time of first goal (mins)	Avg no. of corners
	14th Aug	Newcastle	0 - 1	8	---LL-DDLLWL	8	15	5	►	1	2	2	2-2 (2x)	35	5
	22nd Aug	Arsenal	1 - 4	9	D--DL-DLWLLL	9	18	5	►	1	3	1	1-1 (3x)	40	1
	25th Aug	Fulham	2 - 3	3	---------LLL	3	6	2	►	0	0	2	3-2 (1x)	9	4
	28th Aug	C Palace	n/a	1	L-----------	0	1	0	►	0	0	0	0-1 (1x)	N/A	14
	11th Sep	Birmingham	5 - 3	2	----------WW	6	3	2	►	2	0	0	5-3 (1x)	17	4
	18th Sep	Everton	1 - 1	9	D--LW-LWDLLD	10	19	3	►	1	1	1	2-2 (2x)	37	4
	25th Sep	Chelsea	1 - 2	9	D--WW-DLWLDL	6	6	4	►	3	1	0	1-0 (2x)	48	5
	2nd Oct	Man Utd	3 - 2	9	L--LD-WLLWLW	11	16	5	►	3	1	1	2-3 (2x)	23	3
	16th Oct	Blackburn	2 - 2	7	D--LD-D--WLD	4	5	1	►	1	0	0	1-0 (2x)	36	3
	23rd Oct	Portsmouth	0 - 0	1	----------D	0	0	0	►	0	0	0	0-0 (1x)	N/A	5
	30th Oct	Charlton	0 - 1	5	------D-LDLL	1	4	0	►	0	0	0	1-0 (3x)	74	4
	7th Nov	Bolton	2 - 0	4	---L-----DWW	6	5	3	►	2	1	0	2-0 (2x)	26	7
	14th Nov	West Brom	n/a	1	----------L-	0	1	0	►	0	0	0	1-0 (1x)	N/A	8
	20th Nov	Liverpool	0 - 0	9	L--WD-LWWLWD	11	11	4	►	4	0	0	1-0 (3x)	42	5
	27th Nov	Tottenham	0 - 0	9	D--DL-WWDLWD	13	8	4	►	2	1	1	0-3 (2x)	32	6
	6th Dec	Man City	2 - 1	5	W--W----D-WW	12	4	3	►	3	0	0	4-1 (1x)	34	5
	11th Dec	Southampton	1 - 0	9	L--LL-DDWDDW	11	14	5	►	2	1	2	2-1 (2x)	42	4
	18th Dec	Aston Villa	1 - 2	9	L--LW-DLDWLL	11	20	3	►	2	0	1	3-2 (1x)	47	6
	26th Dec	Birmingham	1 - 3	2	----------LL	1	6	0	►	0	0	0	3-1 (1x)	75	4

Home fixture

Date	Opposition	03-04 scoreline	Played	Premiership history	Goals for	Goals against	No. of times ⚽	►	W	D	L	Most common score (no. times)	Avg time of first goal (mins)	Avg no. of corners	
28th Dec	Norwich	n/a	1	D-----------	3	3	0	►	0	0	0	3-3 (1x)	34	4	
1st Jan	Man Utd	0 - 1	9	D--LD-LLLLWL	9	16	2	►	1	0	1	0-1 (3x)	37	5	
3rd Jan	Chelsea	0 - 0	9	L--LL-LDLDLD	4	18	0	►	0	0	0	1-0 (2x)	51	4	
15th Jan	Everton	1 - 0	9	L--LW-DWLWDW	13	12	5	►	3	1	1	1-2 (2x)	33	6	
22nd Jan	Norwich	n/a	1	D-----------	1	1	1	►	0	1	0	1-1 (1x)	64	4	
1st Feb	Portsmouth	1 - 5	1	----------L	1	5	0	►	0	0	0	5-1 (1x)	27	3	
5th Feb	Blackburn	0 - 1	7	W--WW-W--LWL	11	8	3	►	3	0	0	2-1 (2x)	67	7	
12th Feb	Bolton	0 - 2	4	---D-----LLL	2	6	0	►	0	0	0	2-1 (1x)	69	4	
26th Feb	Charlton	0 - 0	5	------W-DDDD	3	1	1	►	1	0	0	0-0 (3x)	46	6	
5th Mar	Aston Villa	2 - 0	9	L--DL-LLDDLW	5	12	1	►	1	0	0	1-0 (3x)	56	4	
19th Mar	Southampton	3 - 1	9	W--DL-WWLLDW	14	11	3	►	3	0	0	0-1 (2x)	43	5	
2nd Apr	C Palace	n/a	1	L-----------	1	4	0	►	0	0	0	4-1 (1x)	87	6	
9th Apr	Arsenal	0 - 4	9	W--LL-LWLLLL	6	23	2	►	2	0	0	0-4 (2x)	51	3	
16th Apr	Newcastle	1 - 2	8	---LL-DLWLLL	6	15	3	►	1	1	1	2-1 (2x)	60	4	
19th Apr	Fulham	2 - 1	3	---------WDW	6	4	3	►	2	1	0	2-1 (2x)	24	8	
23rd Apr	West Brom	n/a	1	----------W-	3	0	1	►	1	0	0	3-0 (1x)	36	3	
30th Apr	Liverpool	0 - 2	9	L--LL-LDDLDL	4	18	1	►	0	1	0	2-0 (2x)	60	4	
7th May	Tottenham	- 0	9	W--LL-DWDDWW	13	8	3	►	3	0	0	1-1 (2x)	43	8	
14th May	Man City	1 - 0	5	W--W----D-DW	4	1	4	►	3	1	0	0-1 (3x)	36	4	

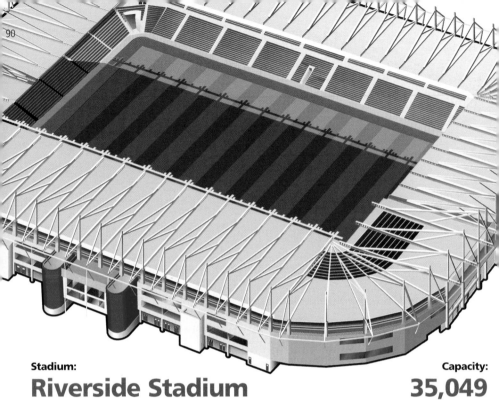

Stadium: **Capacity:**

Riverside Stadium   **35,049**

Useful Information

Website: **www.mfc.co.uk**
Address: **Riverside Stadium,
Middlesbrough, Cleveland TS3 6RS**
Main Switchboard: **01642 877700**

Travel Information

Car Parking: There are various
multi-storey car parks in the town
centre, which fans are encouraged
to use and walk to the ground from,
approx 15 minutes away.
By Train: Middlesbrough station is
about 15 minutes walk from the
ground, take the back exit from
the station, turn right, then after a
couple of minutes right again into
Windward Way.
By Bus: The numbers 36, 37 and 38
go from the town centre to within a short
walking distance of the ground.

Seating Plan

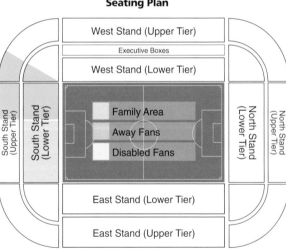

Area Map

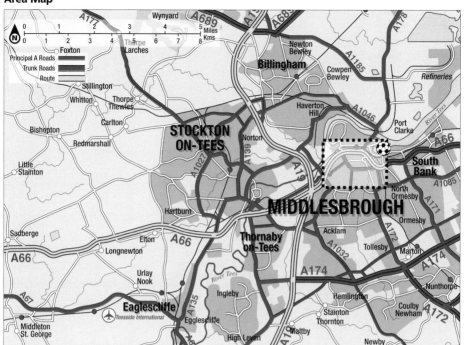

Local Map

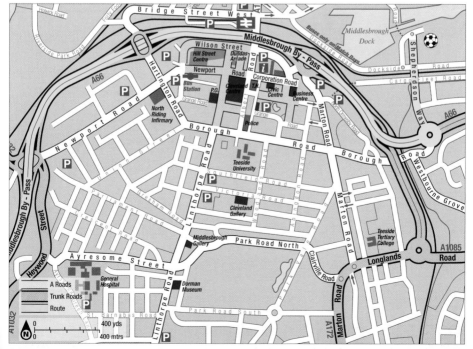

Newcastle United

Manager: **Sir Bobby Robson**

Club Honours and Records
Football League: 1904-05, 1906-07, 1908-09, 1926-27
Division 1: 1992-93
Division 2: 1964-65
FA Cup: 1910, 1924, 1932, 1951, 1952, 1955
Anglo-Italian Cup: 1972-73
Texaco Cup: 1974, 1975
Fairs Cup: 1968-69

Five Season Form

Games Won	Games Drawn	Games Lost	Goals For	Goals Against	Goal Difference
44%	26%	30%	215	244	-29

Ten Season Form

Prem

94-95 95-96 96-97 97-98 98-99 99-00 00-01 01-02 02-03 03-04

Squad List (stats from 2003-04 season)

Position		Appearances	Apps as Sub	Goals/Clean Sheets	Assists	Yellow Cards	Red Cards
G	S.Given	38		11		1	
D	O.Bernard	35		1	5	4	
D	T.Bramble	27	2			7	
D	M.Brittain		1				
D	S.Caldwell	3	2			1	
D	A.Griffin	5				2	
D	A.Hughes	34			1		
D	A.O'Brien	27	1	1		2	2
D	S.Taylor	1					
D	J.Woodgate	18			3		
M	D.Ambrose	10	14	2	3	3	
M	L.Bowyer	17	7	2	3	5	
M	K.Dyer	25		1	5	1	
M	J.Jenas	26	5	2	3	3	
M	L.Robert	31	4	6	10	1	1
M	N.Solano	8	4		3		
M	G.Speed	37	1	3	3	6	
M	H.Viana	5	11		1	2	
F	S.Ameobi	18	8	7	4		
F	C.Bellamy	13	3	4		3	
F	M.Bridges		6			1	
F	M.Chopra	1	5				
F	L.Lua Lua	2	5		1		
F	A.Shearer	37		22	5	1	

S.Given

T.Bramble
J.Woodgate

O.Bernard
A.Hughes

A.O'Brien
J.Woodgate

A.Hughes
A.Griffin

G.Speed
J.Jenas

L.Robert
L.Bowyer
H.Viana

J.Jenas
K.Dyer
L.Bowyer

K.Dyer
D.Ambrose
L.Bowyer
N.Solano

A.Shearer
S.Ameobi

S.Ameobi
C.Bellamy
K.Dyer
L.Lua Lua

Top Goalscorer
Alan Shearer

22 Goals

	Left Foot	Right Foot	Header
Total	-	17	5

% of team's goals **42%**

Goal Breakdown
(stats from 2003-04 season)

	Set Piece	Open Play	Total
Alan Shearer	13	9	**22**
Shola Ameobi	-	7	**7**
Laurent Robert	-	6	**6**
Craig Bellamy	-	4	**4**
Gary Speed	1	2	**3**
Lee Bowyer	-	2	**2**
Jermaine Jenas	-	2	**2**
Darren Ambrose	1	1	**2**
Kieron Dyer	-	1	**1**
Andy O'Brien	1	-	**1**
Olivier Bernard	-	1	**1**

Premiership Statistics
First Goal Scored (average)

Home	Away
25 mins	**22** mins

First Goal Conceded (average)

Home	Away
28 mins	**39** mins

Clean Sheets	Failed To Score
11	**11** matches

Corners Per Game (average)	Average shots on target
6	**5**

Most Common Result:
1-1 (nine times)

Most First Goals:
8 - Alan Shearer

Hat-Tricks:
None

Fastest Goal (mins):
2 - Alan Shearer v Charlton (H)

Fastest Booking (mins):
8 - Lee Bowyer v Aston Villa (H)

Highest Attendance:
52,165 v Man Utd 23/08/03

Lowest Attendance:
42,155 v Everton 03/04/04

Average Attendance: 51,439

Season Progression

18 — 19 — 8 — 6 — 7 — 6 — 4 — 5 — 5 — 5

	Pos		W	D	L	Pts
	5	Newcastle	13	17	8	56

AUG SEPT OCT NOV DEC JAN FEB MAR APR MAY

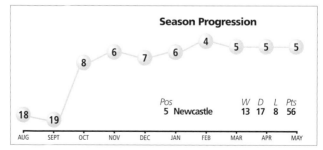

Newcastle United

Enhanced Fixture List 2004-05

In this fixture...

	Date	Opposition	03-04 scoreline	Played	Premiership history	Goals for	Goals against	No. of times ⚽	►	W	D	L	Most common score (no. times)	Avg time of first goal (mins)	Avg no. corn.
	14th Aug	Middlesbro	1 - 0	8	---WW-DDWWWLW	15	8	3	►	3	0	0	2-2 (2x)	32	4
	21st Aug	Tottenham	4 - 0	11	-LDDWWDWWLWW	23	11	7	►	6	1	0	2-1 (2x)	37	8
	25th Aug	Norwich	n/a	2	-WW---------	6	0	2	►	2	0	0	3-0 (2x)	23	6
	28th Aug	Aston Villa	0 - 0	11	-WWDDWLWDDWD	12	6	7	►	5	2	0	1-1 (3x)	53	5
	11th Sep	Blackburn	0 - 1	9	-DDWWDD--WWL	14	8	5	►	3	2	0	1-1 (4x)	47	7
	19th Sep	Southampton	3 - 3	11	-LLLDLLLLLDD	13	25	6	►	0	3	3	2-1 (3x)	41	5
	25th Sep	West Brom	n/a	1	----------W-	2	1	0	►	0	0	0	2-1 (1x)	45	11
	2nd Oct	Birmingham	1 - 1	2	----------WD	3	1	2	►	1	1	0	1-1 (1x)	36	7
	17th Oct	Charlton	0 - 0	5	------D-LDWD	5	5	3	►	1	2	0	2-2 (1x)	40	7
	23rd Oct	Man City	3 - 0	6	-WDW----L-WW	10	2	4	►	4	0	0	2-0 (2x)	26	8
	31st Oct	Bolton	0 - 1	5	---W-L---WLL	10	7	2	►	2	0	0	1-0 (2x)	22	6
	6th Nov	Fulham	3 - 1	3	---------DWW	6	2	3	►	2	1	0	3-1 (1x)	11	7
	14th Nov	Man Utd	1 - 2	11	-DDLWLLWDWLL	19	18	6	►	3	0	3	1-1 (3x)	36	5
	20th Nov	C Palace	n/a	2	--W--W------	3	1	2	►	2	0	0	1-2 (1x)	67	5
	28th Nov	Everton	4 - 2	11	-WWWWWLDLWWW	23	11	6	►	5	1	0	1-0 (3x)	50	6
	4th Dec	Chelsea	0 - 5	11	-LDLDLDLLDLL	5	19	1	►	0	0	1	1-1 (4x)	54	4
	11th Dec	Portsmouth	3 - 0	1	----------W	3	0	1	►	1	0	0	3-0 (1x)	17	5
	18th Dec	Liverpool	1 - 1	11	-WLLLLLLLLDD	14	26	3	►	1	1	1	4-3 (2x)	41	3
	26th Dec	Blackburn	1 - 1	9	-LLLLLD--DLD	6	14	2	►	0	1	1	1-0 (4x)	57	5

Home fixture

Date	Opposition	03-04 scoreline	Played	Premiership history	Goals for	Goals against	No. of times Newcastle scored first and the result that followed ⚽ ▶ W D L			Most common score (no. times)	Avg time of first goal (mins)	Avg no. of corners	Home
28th Dec	Arsenal	0 - 0	11	-WWWLLDWDLDD	12	9	4 ▶ 4	0	0	2-0 (2x)	42	6	
1st Jan	Birmingham	0 - 1	2	----------WL	1	1	1 ▶ 1	0	0	1-0 (1x)	42	9	▦
3rd Jan	West Brom	n/a	1	----------D-	2	2	1 ▶ 0	1	0	2-2 (1x)	43	8	
15th Jan	Southampton	1 - 0	11	-LWWLWWWDWWW	25	8	7 ▶ 6	1	0	2-1 (2x)	28	7	▦
22nd Jan	Arsenal	2 - 3	11	-LWLWLLDLWLL	11	22	2 ▶ 2	0	0	5-0 (1x)	46	4	
2nd Feb	Man City	0 - 1	6	-LDD----W-LL	5	7	2 ▶ 1	0	1	1-0 (2x)	46	7	
5th Feb	Charlton	3 - 1	5	------D-LWWW	8	3	2 ▶ 2	0	0	3-1 (1x)	20	8	▦
12th Feb	Fulham	3 - 2	3	---------LLW	5	7	1 ▶ 0	0	1	3-1 (1x)	40	7	
26th Feb	Bolton	0 - 0	5	---W-W---WWD	8	4	3 ▶ 3	0	0	2-1 (2x)	14	10	▦
5th Mar	Liverpool	1 - 1	11	-WDWDLLDWLWD	15	15	8 ▶ 4	3	1	1-1 (3x)	22	6	▦
19th Mar	Portsmouth	1 - 1	1	-----------D	1	1	1 ▶ 0	1	0	1-1 (1x)	34	6	
2nd Apr	Aston Villa	1 - 1	11	-WWWWWWLWWDD	24	9	7 ▶ 6	1	0	3-0 (2x)	26	7	▦
9th Apr	Tottenham	0 - 1	11	-WLDWLLLLWWL	14	20	4 ▶ 2	0	2	4-2 (2x)	45	7	
16th Apr	Middlesbro	2 - 1	8	---WW-DWLWWW	15	6	5 ▶ 5	0	0	2-1 (2x)	45	9	▦
19th Apr	Norwich	n/a	2	-WL---------	3	3	0 ▶ 0	0	0	2-1 (1x)	30	12	
23rd Apr	Man Utd	0 - 0	11	-DLLDDDLLLLD	7	21	1 ▶ 0	1	0	2-0 (3x)	43	3	
30th Apr	C Palace	n/a	2	--W--L------	4	4	1 ▶ 1	0	0	3-2 (1x)	42	7	▦
7th May	Everton	2 - 2	11	-WLWLDLWDWLD	14	12	6 ▶ 4	2	0	2-0 (2x)	40	4	
14th May	Chelsea	2 - 1	11	-DWWWWLLDLWW	17	10	5 ▶ 5	0	0	3-1 (2x)	30	7	▦

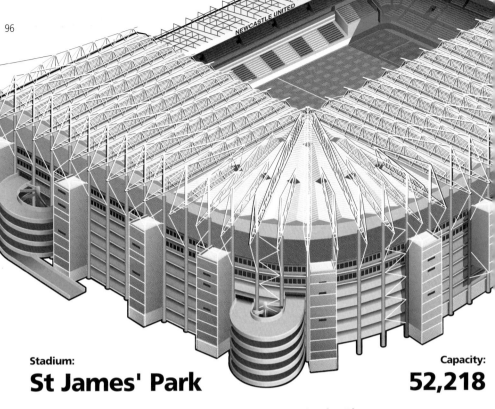

Stadium:

St James' Park

Useful Information

Website: **www.nufc.co.uk**
Address: **St James' Park,**
Newcastle-upon-Tyne NE1 4ST
Main Switchboard: **0191 201 8400**

Travel Information

Car Parking: There is no parking within the confines of St. James' Park. However, there are extensive parking facilities in the City Centre which is a very short walk to the stadium.

By Train: St James' Park is a short 5 minute walk from the British Rail Central Station. Turn left out of the station onto Neville Street, past two sets of lights and right into St James' Boulevard. You will be able to see St. James' Park ahead of you at the top of St. James' Boulevard. The stadium is also served by its own Metro station adjacent to the ground (St James' Metro).

By Bus: Catch a bus from the town centre heading towards Gallowgate.

Seating Plan

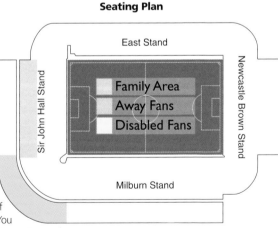

Area Map

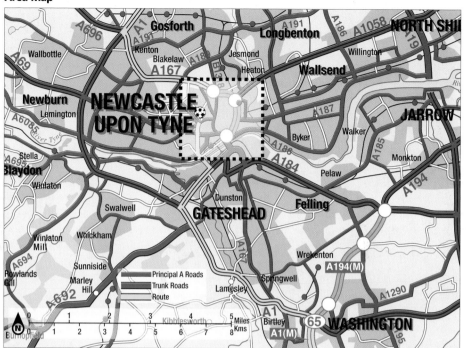

Local Map

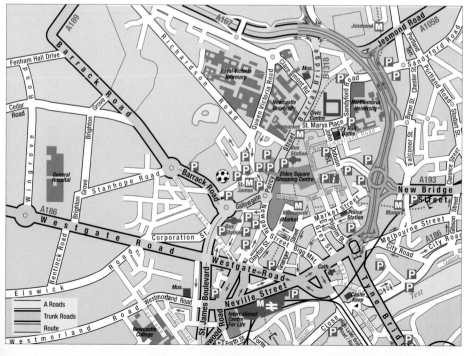

Norwich City
Manager: **Nigel Worthington**

Club Honours and Records
Division 1: 2003-04
Division 2: 1971-71, 1985-86
Division 3 (South): 1933-34
League Cup: 1962

Five Season Form

Games Won	Games Drawn	Games Lost	Goals For	Goals Against	Goal Difference
42%	25%	33%	211	247	-36

Ten Season Form

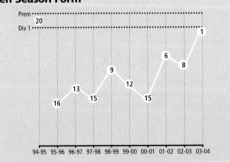

Squad List (stats from 2003-04 season)

Position	Player	Appearances	Apps as Sub	Goals/Clean Sheets	Assists	Yellow Cards	Red Cards
G	R.Green	46		18		1	
D	J.Brennan	7	8	1			
D	K.Briggs	1	2				
D	A.Drury	42			3	3	
D	M.Edworthy	42	1		1	5	
D	C.Fleming	46		3	3	3	
D	M.Mackay	45		4	2	3	1
D	J.Shackell	4	2				
M	K.Cooper	6	4		3	2	
M	C.Easton	8	2	2		1	
M	D.Francis	39	2	7	4	6	
M	K.Harper	9			2	2	1
M	G.Holt	46		1	5	5	
M	P.Mulryne	14	20	3	6	4	
M	A.Notman		1				
M	M.Rivers	7	5	4	1	2	
F	Z.Abbey	1	2				
F	P.Crouch	14	1	4	2	2	1
F	E.Hammond		4				
F	I.Henderson	14	5	4	5	4	
F	D.Huckerby	36		14	18	5	
F	R.Jarvis		12	1			
F	L.McKenzie	12	6	9	4	2	
F	P.McVeigh	36	8	5	7	4	
F	D.Nielsen	2			1	1	
F	I.Roberts	13	28	8		4	
F	M.Svensson	16	4	7	1	3	

On the pitch:

R.Green

M.Mackay
J.Shackell

A.Drury
J.Shackell

C.Fleming

P.McVeigh
C.Easton
J.Brennan

M.Edworthy
G.Holt

G.Holt
P.Mulryne

D.Francis
P.Mulryne

I.Henderson
P.McVeigh
K.Harper
M.Rivers

D.Huckerby
L.McKenzie
P.McVeigh

M.Svensson
P.Crouch
I.Roberts

Top Goalscorer
Darren Huckerby

14 Goals

	Left Foot	Right Foot	Header
Total	3	11	-

% of team's goals **18%**

Goal Breakdown
(stats from 2003-04 season)

	Set Piece	Open Play	Total
Darren Huckerby	3	11	**14**
Leon McKenzie	4	5	**9**
Iwan Roberts	2	6	**8**
Damien Francis	3	4	**7**
Matthias Svensson	-	7	**7**
Paul McVeigh	1	4	**5**
Mark Rivers	2	2	**4**
Malky Mackay	3	1	**4**
Peter Crouch	-	4	**4**
Ian Henderson	-	4	**4**
Craig Fleming	1	2	**3**
Phil Mulryne	-	3	**3**
Clint Easton	-	2	**2**
Jim Brennan	-	1	**1**
Gary Holt	-	1	**1**
Ryan Jarvis	-	1	**1**

League Statistics

First Goal Scored (average)

Home	Away
36 mins	**30** mins

First Goal Conceded (average)

Home	Away
26 mins	**25** mins

Clean Sheets	Failed To Score
18	**9** matches

Corners Per Game (average)	Average shots on target
6	**7**

Most Common Result:
1-0 (seven times)

Most First Goals:
7 - Darren Huckerby

Hat-Tricks:
None

Fastest Goal (mins):
2 - Leon McKenzie v Preston (H)
2 - Damien Francis v Walsall (H)

Fastest Booking (mins):
6 - David Nielsen v Bradford (A)

Highest Attendance:
23,942 v Ipswich Town 07/03/04

Lowest Attendance:
16,082 v Wimbledon 26/08/03

Average Attendance: 18,986

Season Progression

12   4   3   2   1   1   1   1   1   1

Pos		W	D	L	Pts
1	Norwich	28	10	8	94

AUG   SEPT   OCT   NOV   DEC   JAN   FEB   MAR   APR   MAY

Enhanced Fixture List 2004-05

In this fixture...

	Date	Opposition	03-04 scoreline	Played	Premiership history	Goals for	Goals against	No. of times Norwich scored first and the result that followed ⚽	►	W	D	L	Most common score (no. times)	Avg time of first goal (mins)	Avg no. corners
	14th Aug	C Palace	n/a	2	W-D---------	4	2	0	►	0	0	0	4-2 (1x)	9	10
	21st Aug	Man Utd	n/a	3	LDL---------	2	4	0	►	0	0	0	1-0 (2x)	31	4
	25th Aug	Newcastle	n/a	2	-LL---------	0	6	0	►	0	0	0	3-0 (2x)	N/A	5
	28th Aug	Arsenal	n/a	3	DDD---------	2	2	1	►	0	1	0	1-1 (2x)	46	2
	12th Sep	Tottenham	n/a	3	LWL---------	4	7	1	►	1	0	0	5-1 (1x)	56	6
	18th Sep	Aston Villa	n/a	3	WLD---------	3	3	2	►	1	0	1	1-2 (1x)	54	5
	25th Sep	Liverpool	n/a	3	LWL---------	2	8	2	►	1	0	1	4-1 (1x)	19	5
	2nd Oct	Portsmouth	n/a	These teams have never played each other in the Premiership											
	16th Oct	West Brom	n/a	These teams have never played each other in the Premiership											
	23rd Oct	Everton	n/a	3	DWD---------	4	1	1	►	1	0	0	3-0 (1x)	54	4
	1st Nov	Man City	n/a	3	LDL---------	2	6	1	►	0	1	0	3-1 (1x)	36	5
	6th Nov	Blackburn	n/a	3	DDW---------	4	3	0	►	0	0	0	2-2 (1x)	35	4
	13th Nov	Charlton	n/a	These teams have never played each other in the Premiership											
	20th Nov	Southampton	n/a	3	WLD---------	7	7	2	►	1	0	1	4-5 (1x)	54	8
	27th Nov	Birmingham	n/a	These teams have never played each other in the Premiership											
	4th Dec	Fulham	n/a	These teams have never played each other in the Premiership											
	11th Dec	Bolton	n/a	These teams have never played each other in the Premiership											
	18th Dec	Chelsea	n/a	3	WWL---------	5	5	1	►	1	0	0	2-3 (1x)	35	4
	26th Dec	Tottenham	n/a	3	DLL---------	1	4	0	►	0	0	0	1-2 (1x)	70	8

Home fixture

Date	Opposition	03-04 scoreline	Played	Premiership history	Goals for	Goals against	⚽	►	W	D	L	Most common score (no. times)	Avg time of first goal (mins)	Avg no. of corners	
28th Dec	Middlesbro	n/a	1	D-----------	3	3	1	►	0	1	0	3-3 (1x)	14	2	
1st Jan	Portsmouth	n/a		These teams have never played each other in the Premiership											
3rd Jan	Liverpool	n/a	3	WDL---------	4	4	2	►	1	1	0	2-2 (1x)	30	6	
15th Jan	Aston Villa	n/a	3	WDD---------	4	3	2	►	1	1	0	2-3 (1x)	33	5	
22nd Jan	Middlesbro	n/a	1	D-----------	1	1	0	►	0	0	0	1-1 (1x)	86	13	🔲
2nd Feb	Everton	n/a	3	WWL---------	7	3	1	►	1	0	0	2-1 (1x)	47	4	
5th Feb	West Brom	n/a		These teams have never played each other in the Premiership											🔲
12th Feb	Blackburn	n/a	3	LWD---------	4	9	0	►	0	0	0	7-1 (1x)	42	3	
26th Feb	Man City	n/a	3	WDD---------	4	3	3	►	1	2	0	1-1 (2x)	56	4	🔲
5th Mar	Chelsea	n/a	3	WDW---------	6	2	1	►	1	0	0	3-0 (1x)	46	6	🔲
19th Mar	Bolton	n/a		These teams have never played each other in the Premiership											
2nd Apr	Arsenal	n/a	3	WDL---------	5	7	0	►	0	0	0	5-1 (1x)	51	3	
9th Apr	Man Utd	n/a	3	LLL---------	1	7	0	►	0	0	0	0-2 (2x)	60	6	🔲
16th Apr	C Palace	n/a	2	W-W---------	3	1	2	►	2	0	0	1-2 (1x)	32	3	
19th Apr	Newcastle	n/a	2	-LW---------	3	3	2	►	1	0	1	2-1 (1x)	3	6	🔲
23rd Apr	Charlton	n/a		These teams have never played each other in the Premiership											🔲
30th Apr	Southampton	n/a	3	LWD---------	2	4	2	►	1	1	0	3-0 (1x)	47	8	
7th May	Birmingham	n/a		These teams have never played each other in the Premiership											🔲
14th May	Fulham	n/a		These teams have never played each other in the Premiership											

Stadium:

Carrow Road

Capacity:

23,900

Useful Information
Website: www.canaries.co.uk
Address: Carrow Road,
Norwich NR1 1JE
Main Switchboard:
01603 760 760

Travel Information
Car Parking: There are
designated car parks is
the surrounding area.
By Train: Norwich
station in within walking
distance (approx 10
minutes) of Carrow Road.

Seating Plan

South Stand

Family Area
Away Fans
Disabled Fans

Barclay Stand
Upper
Lower

Lower
Executive Boxes
Upper

Norwich and
Peterborough Stand

Goffrey Watling City Stand

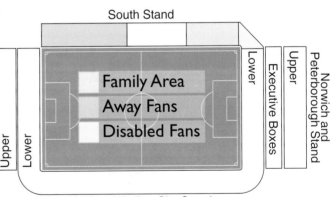

Area Map

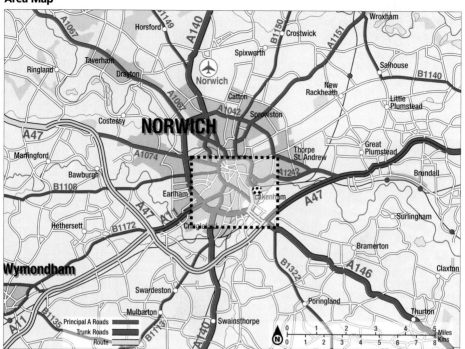

Local Map

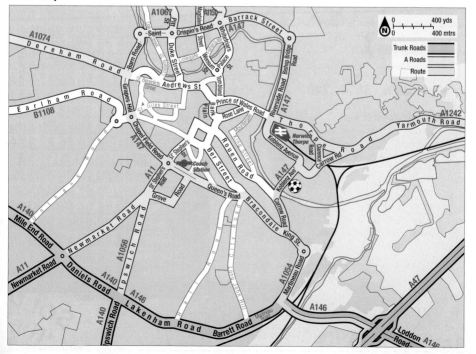

Portsmouth

Manager: **Harry Redknapp**

Club Honours and Records
Football League: 1948-49, 1949-50
Division 1: 2002-03
Division 3: 1961-62, 1982-83
Division 3 (South): 1923-34
FA Cup: 1939

Five Season Form

Games Won	Games Drawn	Games Lost	Goals For	Goals Against	Goal Difference
35%	**29%**	**36%**	**240**	**296**	**-56**

Ten Season Form

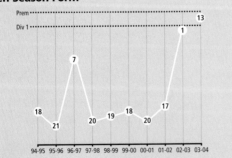

		Prem
		13
Div 1		1

7
18
21
20
19
18
20
17

94-95 95-96 96-97 97-98 98-99 99-00 00-01 01-02 02-03 03-04

Squad List (stats from 2003-04 season)

Position		Appearances	Apps as Sub	Goals/Clean Sheets	Assists	Yellow Cards	Red Cards
G	S.Hislop	30		6		1	
G	P.Srnicek	3		1			
G	H.Wapenaar	5		1			
D	J.Curtis	5	1				
D	A.De Zeeuw	36		1	2	7	
D	R.Duffy		1				
D	H.Foxe	8	2	1		2	
D	P.Pasanen	11	1			1	
D	L.Primus	19	2				
D	S.Schemmel	12	2		1	5	
D	D.Stefanovic	32		3		4	1
D	M.Taylor	18	12		6	2	
D	B.Zivkovic	17	1		1	3	
M	P.Berger	20		5	6	3	1
M	E.Berkovic	10	1	1	1	2	
M	A.Faye	27				6	
M	K.Harper		7				
M	R.Hughes	8	3			1	
M	G.O'Neil	3		2			
M	N.Quashie	17	4	1		5	
M	C.Robinson		1				
M	T.Sherwood	7	6		1	6	
M	A.Smertin	23	3			2	
M	S.Stone	29	3	2	5	2	1
F	Yakubu	35	2	16	11	2	
F	D.Burton		1				
F	L.Lua Lua	10	5	4		1	
F	I.Mornar	3	5	1			
F	V.Pericard		6		1	1	
F	J.Roberts	4	6	1			
F	T.Sheringham	25	7	9	4	5	
F	S.Todorov	1					

S.Hislop
H.Wapenaar
P.Srnicek

M.Taylor
B.Zivkovic
D.Stefanovic

D.Stefanovic
L.Primus

A.De Zeeuw
L.Primus
H.Foxe
P.Pasanen

P.Berger
R.Hughes
N.Quashie
M.Taylor

S.Schemmel
L.Primus
B.Zivkovic

A.Smertin
N.Quashie
E.Berkovic

A.Faye
T.Sherwood

S.Stone
A.Smertin

Yakubu
J.Roberts
S.Todorov

T.Sheringham
L.Lua Lua
I.Mornar
J.Roberts

Top Goalscorer
Yakubu

16 Goals

	Left Foot	Right Foot	Header
Total	**3**	**11**	**2**

7 of team's goals **34%**

Goal Breakdown

(stats from 2003-04 season)

	Set Piece	Open Play	Total
Yakubu	4	12	**16**
Teddy Sheringham	4	5	**9**
Patrik Berger	2	3	**5**
L T Lua Lua	2	2	**4**
Dejan Stefanovic	3	-	**3**
Steve Stone	-	2	**2**
Gary O'Neil	-	2	**2**
Nigel Quashie	-	1	**1**
Eyal Berkovic	-	1	**1**
Arjan De Zeeuw	1	-	**1**
Jason Roberts	-	1	**1**
Hayden Foxe	-	1	**1**
Ivica Mornar	-	1	**1**

Premiership Statistics

First Goal Scored (average)

Home	Away
34	**16**
mins	mins

First Goal Conceded (average)

Home	Away
30	**34**
mins	mins

Clean Sheets	Failed To Score
8	**14**
	matches

Corners Per Game (average)	Average shots on target
5	**4**

Most Common Result:
1-1 (six times)

Most First Goals:
8 - Yakubu

Hat-Tricks:
4 - Yakubu v Middlesbrough (H)
3 - Teddy Sheringham v Bolton (H)

Fastest Goal (mins):
3 - Patrik Berger v Liverpool (H)

Fastest Booking (mins):
2 - Nigel Quashie v Wolves (A)

Highest Attendance:
20,140 v Chelsea 11/02/04

Lowest Attendance:
20,024 v Blackburn 20/09/03

Average Attendance: 20,108

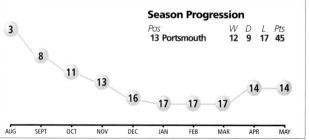

Season Progression

Pos   W   D   L   Pts
13 Portsmouth   12   9   17   45

AUG — 3
SEPT — 8
OCT — 11
NOV — 13
DEC — 16
JAN — 17
FEB — 17
MAR — 17
APR — 14
MAY — 14

Portsmouth

Enhanced Fixture List 2004-05

In this fixture...

	Date	Opposition	03-04 scoreline	Played	Premiership history	Goals for	Goals against	⚽	►	W	D	L	Most common score (no. times)	Avg time of first goal (mins)	Avg no. corners
	14th Aug	Birmingham	3 - 1	1	----------W	3	1	1	►	1	0	0	3-1 (1x)	45	4
	21st Aug	Charlton	1 - 1	1	----------D	1	1	0	►	0	0	0	1-1 (1x)	65	2
	25th Aug	Liverpool	0 - 3	1	----------L	0	3	0	►	0	0	0	3-0 (1x)	N/A	8
	30th Aug	Fulham	1 - 1	1	----------D	1	1	1	►	0	1	0	1-1 (1x)	80	10
	11th Sep	C Palace	n/a		These teams have never played each other in the Premiership										
	18th Sep	Blackburn	2 - 1	1	----------W	2	1	1	►	1	0	0	1-2 (1x)	17	3
	26th Sep	Everton	1 - 2	1	----------L	1	2	1	►	0	0	1	1-2 (1x)	15	7
	2nd Oct	Norwich	n/a		These teams have never played each other in the Premiership										
	18th Oct	Tottenham	2 - 0	1	----------W	2	0	1	►	1	0	0	2-0 (1x)	52	3
	23rd Oct	Middlesbro	0 - 0	1	----------D	0	0	0	►	0	0	0	0-0 (1x)	N/A	5
	30th Oct	Man Utd	1 - 0	1	----------W	1	0	1	►	1	0	0	1-0 (1x)	36	3
	6th Nov	Aston Villa	1 - 2	1	----------L	1	2	0	►	0	0	0	2-1 (1x)	49	6
	13th Nov	Southampton	0 - 3	1	----------L	0	3	0	►	0	0	0	3-0 (1x)	N/A	5
	20th Nov	Man City	4 - 2	1	----------W	4	2	1	►	1	0	0	4-2 (1x)	19	2
	27th Nov	Bolton	0 - 1	1	----------L	0	1	0	►	0	0	0	1-0 (1x)	N/A	2
	4th Dec	West Brom	n/a		These teams have never played each other in the Premiership										
	11th Dec	Newcastle	0 - 3	1	----------L	0	3	0	►	0	0	0	3-0 (1x)	N/A	6
	19th Dec	Arsenal	1 - 1	1	----------D	1	1	1	►	0	1	0	1-1 (1x)	30	5
	26th Dec	C Palace	n/a		These teams have never played each other in the Premiership										

Home fixture

Date	Opposition	03-04 scoreline	Played	Premiership history	Goals for	Goals against	No. of times Portsmouth scored first and the result that followed					Most common score (no. times)	Avg time of first goal (mins)	Avg no. of corners
							⚽	►	W	D	L			
28th Dec	Chelsea	0 - 2	1	----------L	0	2	0	►	0	0	0	0-2 (1x)	N/A	10
1st Jan	Norwich	n/a	These teams have never played each other in the Premiership											
3rd Jan	Everton	0 - 1	1	----------L	0	1	0	►	0	0	0	1-0 (1x)	N/A	4
15th Jan	Blackburn	1 - 2	1	----------L	1	2	0	►	0	0	0	1-2 (1x)	57	8
22nd Jan	Chelsea	0 - 3	1	----------L	0	3	0	►	0	0	0	3-0 (1x)	N/A	1
1st Feb	Middlesbro	5 - 1	1	----------W	5	1	1	►	1	0	0	5-1 (1x)	4	6
5th Feb	Tottenham	3 - 4	1	----------L	3	4	0	►	0	0	0	4-3 (1x)	39	5
12th Feb	Aston Villa	2 - 1	1	----------W	2	1	1	►	1	0	0	2-1 (1x)	42	7
26th Feb	Man Utd	0 - 3	1	----------L	0	3	0	►	0	0	0	3-0 (1x)	N/A	2
5th Mar	Arsenal	1 - 1	1	----------D	1	1	1	►	0	1	0	1-1 (1x)	26	1
19th Mar	Newcastle	1 - 1	1	----------D	1	1	0	►	0	0	0	1-1 (1x)	89	8
2nd Apr	Fulham	0 - 2	1	----------L	0	2	0	►	0	0	0	2-0 (1x)	N/A	11
9th Apr	Charlton	1 - 2	1	----------L	1	2	1	►	0	0	1	1-2 (1x)	34	6
16th Apr	Birmingham	0 - 2	1	----------L	0	2	0	►	0	0	0	2-0 (1x)	N/A	4
19th Apr	Liverpool	1 - 0	1	----------W	1	0	1	►	1	0	0	1-0 (1x)	3	5
23rd Apr	Southampton	1 - 0	1	----------W	1	0	1	►	1	0	0	1-0 (1x)	68	6
30th Apr	Man City	1 - 1	1	----------D	1	1	1	►	0	1	0	1-1 (1x)	24	6
7th May	Bolton	4 - 0	1	----------W	4	0	1	►	1	0	0	4-0 (1x)	48	
14th May	West Brom	n/a	These teams have never played each other in the Premiership											

Stadium:

Fratton Park

Capacity:
19,179

Useful Information
Website: **www.pompeyfc.co.uk**
Address: **Fratton Park, Frogmore Road,
Portsmouth PO4 8RA**
Main Switchboard: **023 9273 1204**

Travel Information
By Train: Fratton station is a
short walk from the ground
By Bus: Numbers 3, 13, 14,
16a, 24, 27 and 57 all run
to Fratton station.

Seating Plan

North Stand

TY Europe Stand

Milton Stand

Family Area
Away Fans
Disabled Fans

South Stand

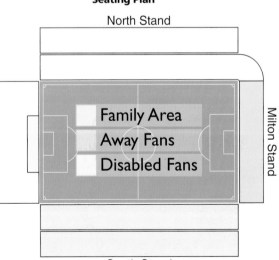

Area Map

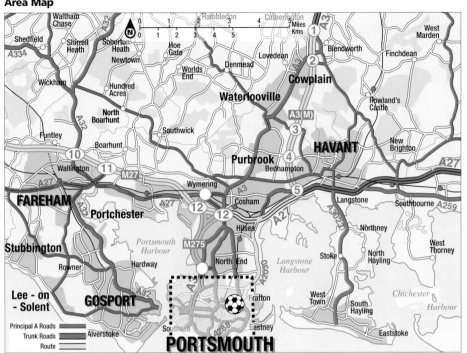

PORTSMOUTH

Principal A Roads
Trunk Roads
Route

Local Map

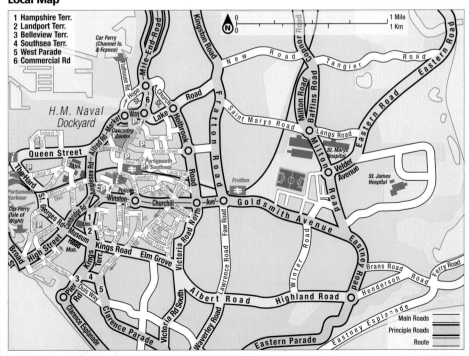

1 Hampshire Terr.
2 Landport Terr.
3 Belleview Terr.
4 Southsea Terr.
5 West Parade
6 Commercial Rd

Main Roads
Principle Roads
Route

Southampton

Manager: **Paul Sturrock**

Club Honours and Records

Division 3: 1959-60
Division 3 (South): 1921-22
FA Cup: 1976

Squad List (stats from 2003-04 season)

Position	Name	Appearances	Apps as Sub	Goals/Clean Sheets	Assists	Yellow Cards	Red Cards
G	A.Blayney	2					
G	P.Jones	8		4			
G	A.Niemi	28		8		1	
D	C.Baird	1	3			1	
D	S.Crainey	5			1		
D	M.Cranie	1					
D	J.Dodd	27	1		4	2	
D	F.Hall	7	4				
D	D.Higginbotham	24	3			3	
D	D.Kenton	3	4				
D	G.Le Saux	19			2	4	
D	C.Lundekvam	31		1	2	2	
D	M.Svensson	26		2	1	6	1
M	R.Delap	26	1	1	3	1	
M	F.Fernandes	21	6	1	3	2	
M	Y.Folly	9				1	
M	L.Griffit	2	3	2			
M	C.Marsden	9	4			4	
M	N.McCann	9	9			4	
M	M.Oakley	7			1	2	
M	D.Prutton	22	5	1	3	4	1
M	A.Svensson	17	13		3	6	
M	P.Telfer	33	4		2	3	
F	J.Beattie	32	5	14	10	3	
F	A.Delgado		4				
F	B.Ormerod	14	8	5		1	
F	M.Pahars	6	8	2	1		
F	K.Phillips	28	6	12	5	2	1
F	J.Tessem	1	2				

Five Season Form

Games Won	Games Drawn	Games Lost	Goals For	Goals Against	Goal Difference
33%	27%	40%	202	255	-53

Ten Season Form

Prem

11 · 17 · 15 · 12 · 17 · 15 · 10 · 11 · 8 · 12

94-95 95-96 96-97 97-98 98-99 99-00 00-01 01-02 02-03 03-04

Formation:

A.Niemi
P.Jones
A.Blayney

G.Le Saux
D.Higginbotham
S.Crainey

M.Svensson
D.Higginbotham
F.Hall

C.Lundekvam
F.Hall
D.Kenton

J.Dodd
P.Telfer

N.McCann
A.Svensson
D.Prutton
M.Pahars

R.Delap
Y.Folly
P.Telfer

D.Prutton
A.Svensson
M.Oakley
Y.Folly

F.Fernandes
P.Telfer

J.Beattie
B.Ormerod

K.Phillips
B.Ormerod

Top Goalscorer
James Beattie

14 Goals

	Left Foot	Right Foot	Header
Total	1	9	4

% of team's goals **32%**

Goal Breakdown
(stats from 2003-04 season)

	Set Piece	Open Play	Total
James Beattie	7	7	**14**
Kevin Phillips	-	12	**12**
Brett Ormerod	2	3	**5**
Marian Pahars	-	2	**2**
Michael Svensson	2	-	**2**
Leandre Griffit	-	2	**2**
Claus Lundekvam	1	-	**1**
Rory Delap	-	1	**1**
David Prutton	-	1	**1**
Fabrice Fernandes	1	-	**1**

Premiership Statistics
First Goal Scored (average)

Home	Away
27 mins	**17** mins

First Goal Conceded (average)

Home	Away
18 mins	**37** mins

Clean Sheets	Failed To Score
12	**16** matches

Corners Per Game (average)	Average shots on target
6	**5**

Most Common Result:
0-0, 0-1 (six times)

Most First Goals:
9 - James Beattie

Hat-Tricks:
None

Fastest Goal (mins):
2 - Brett Ormerod v Liverpool (A)

Fastest Booking (mins):
8 - Jason Dodd v Bolton (A)

Highest Attendance:
32,151 v Arsenal 29/12/03

Lowest Attendance:
30,513 v Charlton 07/12/03

Average Attendance: 31,716

Season Progression

Pos
12 Southampton

W	D	L	Pts
12	11	15	47

8 — 5 — 6 — 11 — 8 — 10 — 12 — 10 — 11 — 12

AUG SEPT OCT NOV DEC JAN FEB MAR APR MAY

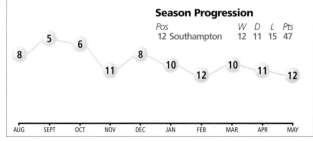

Southampton

Enhanced Fixture List 2004-05

In this fixture...

	Date	Opposition	03-04 scoreline	Played	Premiership history	Goals for	Goals against	⚽	► W	D	L	Most common score (no. times)	Avg time of first goal (mins)	Avg no. of corners
	14th Aug	Aston Villa	0 - 1	12	DWDLLDLWDLWL	8	13	3	► 3	0	0	1-1 (3x)	68	5
	21st Aug	Blackburn	2 - 0	10	DWDWWWWD--LDW	18	9	9	► 5	3	1	1-1 (3x)	34	6
	25th Aug	Bolton	1 - 2	5	---W-L---DDL	2	3	2	► 1	0	1	0-0 (2x)	48	7
	28th Aug	Chelsea	0 - 4	12	DLWLLLLDLWDL	10	20	4	► 2	2	0	1-0 (3x)	23	5
	13th Sep	Charlton	1 - 2	5	------L-DDLL	4	11	1	► 0	1	0	2-1 (2x)	80	8
	19th Sep	Newcastle	3 - 3	11	-WWWDWWWWWDD	25	13	5	► 5	0	0	2-1 (3x)	53	6
	25th Sep	Fulham	0 - 2	3	---------LDL	3	6	0	► 0	0	0	2-2 (1x)	57	6
	2nd Oct	Man City	0 - 2	7	LLDD----L-WL	5	9	3	► 1	2	0	0-2 (2x)	31	8
	16th Oct	Everton	0 - 0	12	LLDLLWLLDLLD	7	22	4	► 1	1	2	2-1 (2x)	41	6
	24th Oct	Birmingham	0 - 0	2	----------WD	2	0	1	► 1	0	0	2-0 (1x)	60	4
	30th Oct	Arsenal	0 - 2	12	LLDLLLDLLDLL	11	30	1	► 0	0	1	1-1 (3x)	53	4
	6th Nov	West Brom	n/a	1	----------W-	1	0	1	► 1	0	0	1-0 (1x)	8	9
	13th Nov	Portsmouth	3 - 0	1	-----------W	3	0	1	► 1	0	0	3-0 (1x)	34	8
	20th Nov	Norwich	n/a	3	LWD---------	7	7	1	► 0	1	0	4-5 (1x)	39	4
	27th Nov	C Palace	n/a	3	W-W--W------	5	1	3	► 3	0	0	1-0 (2x)	36	7
	4th Dec	Man Utd	2 - 3	12	LLLLLLLDLLLL	12	34	4	► 0	1	3	2-1 (5x)	44	5
	11th Dec	Middlesbro	0 - 1	9	W--WW-DDLDDL	14	11	3	► 1	2	0	2-1 (2x)	54	7
	18th Dec	Tottenham	3 - 1	12	LLWLLDLLDLLW	12	28	4	► 1	1	2	3-0 (2x)	31	4
	26th Dec	Charlton	3 - 2	5	------W-DWDW	7	3	3	► 3	0	0	0-0 (2x)	24	7

Home fixture

Date	Opposition	03-04 scoreline	Played	Premiership history	Goals for	Goals against	No. of times Southampton scored first ⚽	▶	W	D	L	Most common score (no. times)	Avg time of first goal (mins)	Avg no. of corners	Home fixture
28th Dec	Liverpool	2 - 1	12	DLLDLWLDLDLW	14	27	5	▶	2	2	1	1-1 (3x)	36	4	
1st Jan	Man City	3 - 1	7	LDDL----W-WW	10	8	5	▶	3	2	0	0-1 (2x)	40	4	
3rd Jan	Fulham	0 - 0	3	---------DWD	5	3	0	▶	0	0	0	4-2 (1x)	24	9	🏠
15th Jan	Newcastle	0 - 1	11	-WLLWLLLDLLL	8	25	4	▶	2	0	2	2-1 (2x)	34	4	
22nd Jan	Liverpool	2 - 0	12	WWLLLDLDDWLW	17	17	7	▶	4	1	2	2-0 (2x)	37	5	🏠
1st Feb	Birmingham	1 - 2	2	----------LL	3	5	2	▶	0	0	2	3-2 (1x)	16	7	
5th Feb	Everton	3 - 3	12	DLWDDWWWWLWD	17	11	7	▶	6	1	0	2-0 (3x)	50	7	🏠
12th Feb	West Brom	n/a	1	----------L-	0	1	0	▶	0	0	0	1-0 (1x)	N/A	7	
26th Feb	Arsenal	0 - 1	12	WLWDLLDLWLWL	10	17	2	▶	2	0	0	3-2 (2x)	38	5	🏠
5th Mar	Tottenham	1 - 0	12	DWWDLWDLWWWW	14	8	6	▶	6	0	0	1-0 (4x)	54	6	🏠
19th Mar	Middlesbro	1 - 3	9	L--DW-LLWWDL	11	14	5	▶	3	1	1	0-1 (2x)	51	3	
2nd Apr	Chelsea	0 - 1	12	WWLLDWLLWLDL	12	15	6	▶	4	1	1	1-0 (2x)	33	6	🏠
9th Apr	Blackburn	1 - 1	10	DLLLLLW--LLD	7	14	2	▶	1	1	0	2-1 (2x)	45	5	
16th Apr	Aston Villa	1 - 1	12	WWWLLLLWWLDD	18	16	5	▶	5	0	0	2-0 (3x)	33	4	🏠
19th Apr	Bolton	0 - 0	5	---W-D---WDD	3	1	3	▶	2	1	0	0-1 (2x)	62	4	
23rd Apr	Portsmouth	0 - 1	1	----------L	0	1	0	▶	0	0	0	1-0 (1x)	N/A	4	
30th Apr	Norwich	n/a	3	WLD--------	4	2	1	▶	1	0	0	3-0 (1x)	49	6	🏠
7th May	C Palace	n/a	3	W-D--D------	3	2	2	▶	1	1	0	1-2 (1x)	42	4	
14th May	Man Utd	1 - 0	12	LLDWWWLLWLLW	18	22	7	▶	5	1	1	1-3 (3x)	29	6	🏠

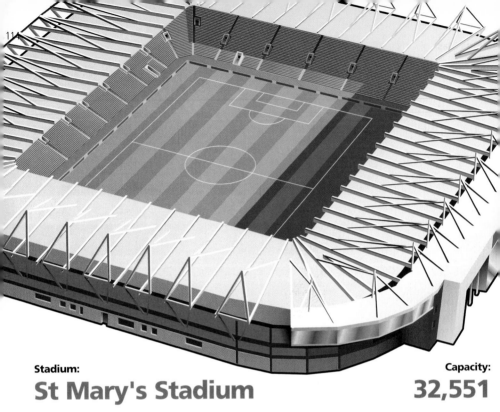

Stadium: **Capacity:**

St Mary's Stadium   ## 32,551

Useful Information
Website: www.saintsfc.co.uk
Address: **The Friends Provident
St Mary's Stadium, Britannia Road,
Southampton, Hants SO14 5FP**
Main Switchboard: **0870 220 0000**

Travel Information
Car Parking: The club urge people
not to head towards the stadium by
car as the surrounding area is subject
to police restrictions. Parking for both
home and visiting supporters may be
available, but bookings must be made
in advance. Please phone 0870 220
0150 for details.
By Tube/Bus: The nearest station to
the ground is Southampton Central.
Shuttle buses run from the station
to the stadium two hours before the game
up until kick off.

Seating Plan

Itchen Stand

Northam Stand

Family Area
Away Fans
Disabled Fans

Chapel Stand

Kingsland Stand

Area Map

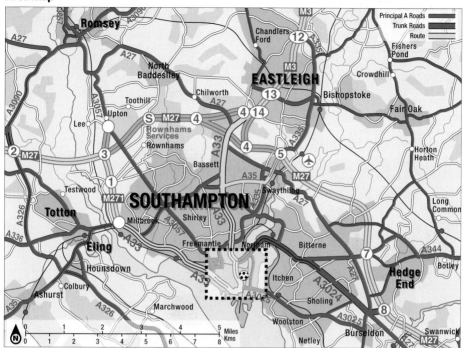

Principal A Roads
Trunk Roads
Route

Romsey
North Baddesley
Chandlers Ford 12
Fishers Pond
A27
A27
M3
Crowdhill
EASTLEIGH
Toothill
Chilworth
A27
13
Bishopstoke
Fair Oak
Upton
Lee
S M27 4
4 14
Horton Heath
Rownhams Services
Rownhams
4
5
Bassett
M27
Testwood
1
A35
Swaythling
Long Common
Totton
M271
SOUTHAMPTON
A27
Millbrook
Shirley
Eling
A33
Freemantle
Northam
Bitterne
7
Botley
A344
Hounsdown
Itchen
Hedge End
Colbury
Ashurst
A326
Marchwood
Sholing
A3024
A3025
8
Woolston
Burseldon
Swanwick
Netley
M27

0 1 2 3 4 5 Miles
0 1 2 3 4 5 6 7 8 Kms
N

Local Map

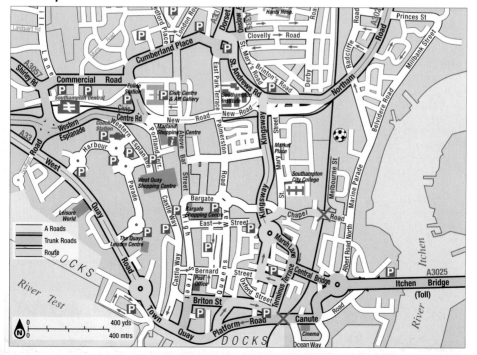

A Roads
Trunk Roads
Route

Landguard Rd
Shirley Rd
A3057
Commercial Road
Southampton Central
Western Esplanade
Harbour Parade
Leisure World
The Quays Leisure Centre
DOCKS
River Test
Town Quay
West Quay Road
Cumberland Place
London Road
Dorset
Hants Hosp.
Clovelly Road
Brinton's Road
Derby Road
Princes St
Millbank Street
Police Station
Civic Centre & Art Gallery
Southampton Institute
St Mary's Rd
Radcliffe Road
Northam Road
St Andrews Rd
East Park Terrace
New Road
Marland Shopping Centre
Portland Terr.
Above Bar Street
Palmerston Road
New Road
Kingsbury
Kingsway
Market Place
Southampton City College
Belvidere Road
Marine Parade
West Quay Shopping Centre
Castle Way
Bargate
Bargate Shopping Centre
High Street
East Street
West Street
Chapel Road
Marsh Lane
Melbourne St
Albert Road North
Castle Way
Bernard Street
Post Office
Queens Terrace
Oxford Street
Terminus Terrace
Central Bridge
Itchen Bridge (Toll)
A3025
Briton St
Town Quay
Platform Road
Canute Road
Ocean Way
Cinema
River Itchen
DOCKS
N
0 400 yds
0 400 mtrs

Tottenham Hotspur

Manager: **Jacques Santini**

Club Honours and Records

Football League: 1950-51, 1960-61
Division 2: 1919-20, 1949-50
FA Cup: 1901, 1921, 1961, 1962, 1967, 1981, 1982, 1991
League Cup: 1971, 1973, 1999
Cup-Winners' Cup: 1962-63
UEFA Cup: 1971-72, 1983-84

Five Season Form

Games Won	Games Drawn	Games Lost	Goals For	Goals Against	Goal Difference
36%	21%	43%	215	275	-60

Ten Season Form

Prem

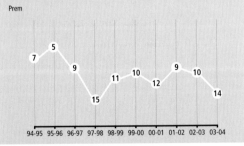

94-95 95-96 96-97 97-98 98-99 99-00 00-01 01-02 02-03 03-04

Squad List (stats from 2003-04 season)

Position		Appearances	Apps as Sub	Goals/Clean Sheets	Assists	Yellow Cards	Red Cards
G	K.Keller	38		8			
D	G.Bunjevcevic	3	4				
D	S.Carr	32		1	3	8	1
D	G.Doherty	16	1			3	
D	A.Gardner	33				8	
D	S.Kelly	7	4				
D	L.King	28	1	1	4	1	
D	P.Konchesky	10	2		1	4	
D	M.Mabizela		6	1		1	
D	D.Richards	23			2	3	
D	M.Taricco	31	1	1	1	9	
D	C.Ziege	7	1			2	
M	D.Anderton	16	4	1	6	4	
M	J.Blondel		1			1	
M	M.Brown	17		1	2	1	
M	S.Dalmat	12	10	3	3	2	
M	S.Davies	17		2	3	2	
M	J.Jackson	9	2	1	2		
M	D.Marney	1	2			1	
M	G.Poyet	12	8	3	1	1	
M	J.Redknapp	14	3	1		6	
M	R.Ricketts	12	12	1	1	1	
F	J.Defoe	14	1	7		1	
F	F.Kanoute	19	8	7	1		
F	R.Keane	31	3	14	8	1	
F	H.Postiga	9	10	1	1	1	
F	M.Yeates	1			1		
F	B.Zamora	6	10		2	1	

K.Keller

M.Taricco
C.Ziege

A.Gardner
G.Doherty

D.Richards
G.Doherty
L.King

R.Ricketts
P.Konchesky
J.Jackson

S.Carr
S.Kelly

J.Redknapp
M.Brown
G.Poyet

L.King
D.Anderton

S.Davies
S.Dalmat
D.Anderton

J.Defoe
F.Kanoute
H.Postiga
B.Zamora

R.Keane
F.Kanoute

Top Goalscorer
Robbie Keane

14 Goals

	Left Foot	Right Foot	Header
Total	3	11	-

% of team's goals **30%**

Goal Breakdown
(stats from 2003-04 season)

	Set Piece	Open Play	Total
Robbie Keane	5	9	**14**
Frederic Kanoute	1	6	**7**
Jermain Defoe		7	**7**
Gustavo Poyet	1	2	**3**
Stephane Dalmat	1	2	**3**
Simon Davies	-	2	**2**
Jamie Redknapp	-	1	**1**
Darren Anderton	-	1	**1**
Stephen Carr	-	1	**1**
Mauricio Taricco	-	1	**1**
Michael Brown	1	-	**1**
Ledley King	-	1	**1**
Johnnie Jackson	-	1	**1**
Rohan Ricketts	-	1	**1**
Mbulelo Mabizela	-	1	**1**
Helder Postiga	-	1	**1**

Premiership Statistics

First Goal Scored (average)

Home	Away
31 mins	**16** mins

First Goal Conceded (average)

Home	Away
28 mins	**33** mins

Clean Sheets	Failed To Score
8	**16** matches

Corners Per Game (average)	Average shots on target
5	**5**

Most Common Result:
0-1 (eight times)

Most First Goals:
5 - Robbie Keane

Hat-Tricks:
Robbie Keane v Wolves (H)

Fastest Goal (mins):
5 - Darren Anderton v Arsenal (A)

Fastest Booking (mins):
9 - Jamie Redknapp
v Liverpool (A)

Highest Attendance:
36,137 v Everton 04/10/03

Lowest Attendance:
30,016 v Birmingham 07/01/04

Average Attendance: 34,876

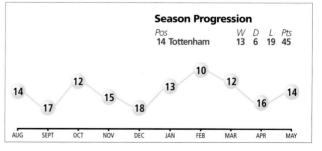

Season Progression

Pos	W	D	L	Pts
14 Tottenham	13	6	19	45

14 — AUG
17 — SEPT
12 — OCT
15 — NOV
18 — DEC
13 — JAN
10 — FEB
12 — MAR
16 — APR
14 — MAY

Tottenham Hotspur

Enhanced Fixture List 2004-05

In this fixture...

Date	Opposition	03-04 scoreline	Played	Premiership history	Goals for	Goals against	⚽	►	W	D	L	Most common score (no. times)	Avg time of first goal (mins)	Avg no. of corners
14th Aug	Liverpool	2 - 1	12	WDDLLDWWWWLW	19	17	8	►	5	2	1	2-1 (3x)	40	6
21st Aug	Newcastle	0 - 4	11	-WDDLLDLLWLL	11	23	4	►	2	2	0	2-1 (2x)	47	4
25th Aug	West Brom	n/a	1	----------W-	3	2	0	►	0	0	0	2-3 (1x)	45	8
28th Aug	Birmingham	4 - 1	2	----------WW	6	2	2	►	2	0	0	4-1 (1x)	9	6
12th Sep	Norwich	n/a	3	WLW---------	7	4	2	►	2	0	0	5-1 (1x)	45	6
19th Sep	Chelsea	2 - 4	12	DLDDLLLLLLDL	9	26	5	►	0	3	2	1-1 (3x)	23	5
25th Sep	Man Utd	1 - 2	12	DLLWLLDWWLLL	18	21	3	►	2	0	1	3-1 (2x)	42	5
2nd Oct	Everton	1 - 3	12	WWDDLWWDDDDL	13	11	5	►	4	1	0	2-2 (2x)	46	3
18th Oct	Portsmouth	0 - 2	1	----------L	0	2	0	►	0	0	0	2-0 (1x)	N/A	7
23rd Oct	Bolton	0 - 1	5	---D-W---WWL	9	6	3	►	2	1	0	3-2 (1x)	51	8
30th Oct	Fulham	1 - 2	3	---------WLL	5	5	3	►	1	0	2	3-2 (1x)	27	8
6th Nov	Charlton	0 - 1	5	------D-DLDL	4	6	0	►	0	0	0	2-2 (2x)	59	7
13th Nov	Arsenal	2 - 2	12	WLWWDDLWDDDD	13	12	6	►	3	3	0	1-1 (4x)	34	4
22nd Nov	Aston Villa	0 - 1	12	DLLLDLLDLDWL	8	17	4	►	1	3	0	1-1 (3x)	51	4
27th Nov	Middlesbro	0 - 0	9	D--DW-LLDWLD	8	13	3	►	1	1	1	0-3 (2x)	63	6
4th Dec	Blackburn	0 - 1	10	WLLLWWD--LWL	12	10	4	►	4	0	0	2-1 (2x)	49	4
11th Dec	Man City	0 - 0	7	WWLD----W-WD	10	8	4	►	3	1	0	0-1 (2x)	55	5
18th Dec	Southampton	1 - 3	12	WWLWWDWWDWWL	28	12	7	►	6	0	1	3-0 (2x)	32	6
26th Dec	Norwich	n/a	3	DWW---------	4	1	2	►	2	0	0	1-2 (1x)	33	3

Home fixture

Date	Opposition	03-04 scoreline	Played	Premiership history	Goals for	Goals against	No. of times Tottenham scored first ⚽	►	W	D	L	Most common score (no. times)	Avg time of first goal (mins)	Avg no. of corners	Home
28th Dec	C Palace	n/a	3	D-D--L------	2	3	1	►	0	1	0	2-2 (1x)	16	9	H
1st Jan	Everton	3 - 0	12	WWWDDDWWWDWW	26	14	4	►	3	1	0	3-2 (3x)	40	9	H
3rd Jan	Man Utd	0 - 3	12	LLDLLLLLLLLL	4	26	1	►	0	0	1	2-0 (3x)	51	4	
15th Jan	Chelsea	0 - 1	12	LDDDLLDLLLDL	9	22	0	►	0	0	0	1-2 (2x)	68	5	H
22nd Jan	C Palace	n/a	3	W-D--W------	7	3	2	►	2	0	0	1-3 (2x)	52	5	
1st Feb	Bolton	0 - 2	5	---W-D---DLL	5	7	2	►	1	1	0	1-1 (2x)	32	5	
5th Feb	Portsmouth	4 - 3	1	-----------W	4	3	1	►	1	0	0	4-3 (1x)	13	6	H
12th Feb	Charlton	4 - 2	5	------W-LLWW	10	7	2	►	2	0	0	3-1 (1x)	40	6	
26th Feb	Fulham	0 - 3	3	---------WDL	5	4	1	►	1	0	0	4-0 (1x)	30	5	H
5th Mar	Southampton	0 - 1	12	DLLDWLDWLLLL	8	14	4	►	2	1	1	1-0 (4x)	46	5	
19th Mar	Man City	1 - 1	7	WWWWW----D-LD	8	5	3	►	3	0	0	1-0 (2x)	53	7	H
2nd Apr	Birmingham	0 - 1	2	----------DL	1	2	1	►	0	1	0	1-1 (1x)	55	3	
9th Apr	Newcastle	1 - 0	11	-LWDLWWWWLLW	20	14	7	►	4	1	2	4-2 (2x)	35	6	H
16th Apr	Liverpool	0 - 0	12	LWDDLLLLLLLD	10	25	2	►	0	0	2	2-1 (2x)	40	4	
20th Apr	West Brom	n/a	1	----------W-	3	1	1	►	1	0	0	3-1 (1x)	3	5	H
23rd Apr	Arsenal	1 - 2	12	WDDDLDDLLLLL	9	17	3	►	1	1	1	2-1 (3x)	45	3	
30th Apr	Aston Villa	2 - 1	12	DDLLWWWLDDWW	14	13	5	►	4	0	1	1-0 (3x)	48	6	H
7th May	Middlesbro	0 - 1	9	L--WW-DLDDLL	8	13	5	►	2	2	1	1-1 (2x)	39	5	
14th May	Blackburn	1 - 0	10	LLWLWDW--WLW	12	14	4	►	4	0	0	2-1 (2x)	42	7	H

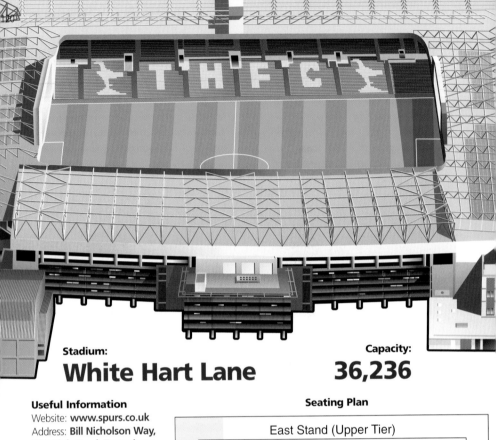

Stadium:

White Hart Lane

Capacity:

36,236

Useful Information

Website: **www.spurs.co.uk**
Address: **Bill Nicholson Way,
748 High Road, Tottenham,
London N17 0AP**
Main Switchboard:
020 8365 5000

Travel Information

Car Parking: Limited parking
is available near the ground.
By Train/Tube: The nearest
Underground station is Seven
Sisters (Victoria Line), approx 30
minutes walk. The nearest station
is White Hart Lane, approx 5
minutes walk, on the Liverpool
Street-Enfield Town line.
By Bus: Numbers 149, 259
and 279 all go along
Tottenham High Road.

Seating Plan

East Stand (Upper Tier)

East Stand (Lower Tier)

North Stand (Upper Tier)

North Stand (Lower Tier)

South Stand (Upper Tier)

South Stand (Lower Tier)

Family Area

Away Fans

Disabled Fans

West Stand (Lower Tier)

West Stand (Upper Tier)

Area Map

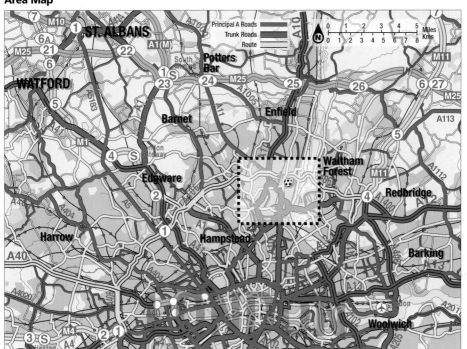

Local Map

West Bromwich Albion

Manager: **Gary Megson**

Club Honours and Records
Division 2: 1901-02, 1910-11
FA Cup: 1888, 1892, 1931, 1954, 1968
League Cup: 1966

Five Season Form

Games Won	Games Drawn	Games Lost	Goals For	Goals Against	Goal Difference
40%	**26%**	**34%**	**221**	**248**	**-27**

Ten Season Form

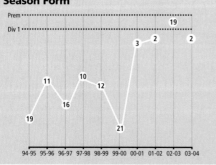

Squad List (stats from 2003-04 season)							
Position		Appearances	Apps as Sub	Goals/Clean Sheets	Assists	Yellow Cards	Red Cards
G	R.Hoult	44		19			
G	J.Murphy	2	1	0			
D	S.Berthe	2	1				
D	J.Chambers	14	3			1	
D	N.Clement	25	10	2	2	1	
D	T.Gaardsoe	45		4	3	5	1
D	P.Gilchrist	16	1		2	1	
D	S.Gregan	40	3	1	1	7	
D	B.Haas	36		1	1	8	
D	D.Moore	20	2	2		1	
D	A.N'Dour	2			1		
D	P.Robinson	30	1		2	5	
D	L.Sigurdsson	5				2	
D	J.Volmer	10	5			1	
M	L.Dyer	2	15	2	3		
M	A.Johnson	33	5	2	5	2	1
M	M.Kinsella	15	3	1		2	
M	J.Koumas	37	5	10	15	4	2
M	J.O'Connor	27	3			4	
M	A.Sakiri	6	19	1	1		
M	R.Wallwork	4	1		1	1	
F	D.Dichio	5	6			1	
F	S.Dobie	14	17	5	4	2	
F	D.Facey	2	7		1		
F	G.Horsfield	20		7	5	2	
F	L.Hughes	21	11	11	4	4	
F	R.Hulse	29	4	10	6	3	1
F	M.Skoubo		2				

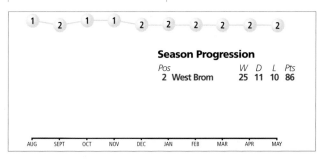

R.Hoult
J.Murphy

S.Gregan
P.Gilchrist
J.Volmer

P.Robinson
N.Clement

D.Moore
T.Gaardsoe

T.Gaardsoe
S.Gregan
L.Sigurdsson

A.Johnson
J.Koumas
A.Saniri
N.Clement

B.Haas
J.Chambers

J.O'Connor
M.Kinsella
S.Gregan

J.Koumas
A.Johnson
S.Gregan

R.Hulse
L.Hughes

G.Horsfield
S.Dobie

Top Goalscorer
Lee Hughes

11 Goals

	Left Foot	Right Foot	Header
Total	1	9	1

% of team's goals **17%**

Goal Breakdown
(stats from 2003-04 season)

	Set Piece	Open Play	Total
Lee Hughes	5	6	**11**
Jason Koumas	3	7	**10**
Rob Hulse	4	6	**10**
Geoff Horsfield		7	**7**
Scott Dobie	1	4	**5**
Thomas Gaardsoe	2	2	**4**
Andy Johnson		2	**2**
Neil Clement	2		**2**
Darren Moore	2		**2**
Lloyd Dyer		2	**2**
Mark Kinsella		1	**1**
Sean Gregan		1	**1**
Bernt Haas	1		**1**
Artim Sakiri		1	**1**

League Statistics

First Goal Scored (average)

Home	Away
36 mins	**43** mins

First Goal Conceded (average)

Home	Away
31 mins	**30** mins

Clean Sheets	Failed To Score
19	**12** matches

Corners Per Game (average)	Average shots on target
6	**6**

Most Common Result:
1-0 (eight times)

Most First Goals:
8 - Jason Koumas

Hat-Tricks:
None

Fastest Goal (mins):
5 - Jason Koumas v Millwall (H)

Fastest Booking (mins):
2 - Paul Robinson
v Gillingham (H)

Highest Attendance:
27,195 v Sheff Utd 14/10/03

Lowest Attendance:
22,048 v Wimbledon 21/10/03

Average Attendance: 24,764

Season Progression

Pos		W	D	L	Pts
2	West Brom	25	11	10	86

AUG SEPT OCT NOV DEC JAN FEB MAR APR MAY

West Bromwich Albion

Enhanced Fixture List 2004-05

In this fixture...

	Date	Opposition	03-04 scoreline	Played	Premiership history	Goals for	Goals against	No of times West Brom scored first and the result that followed ⚽	▶	W	D	L	Most common score (no. times)	Avg time of first goal (mins)	Avg no of first corn
	14th Aug	Blackburn	n/a	1	----------D-	1	1	0	▶	0	0	0	1-1 (1x)	54	2
	22nd Aug	Aston Villa	n/a	1	----------D-	0	0	0	▶	0	0	0	0-0 (1x)	N/A	8
	24th Aug	Tottenham	n/a	1	----------L-	2	3	1	▶	0	0	1	2-3 (1x)	24	5
	28th Aug	Everton	n/a	1	----------L-	0	1	0	▶	0	0	0	1-0 (1x)	N/A	6
	11th Sep	Liverpool	n/a	1	----------L-	0	2	0	▶	0	0	0	2-0 (1x)	N/A	2
	18th Sep	Fulham	n/a	1	----------W-	1	0	1	▶	1	0	0	1-0 (1x)	48	5
	25th Sep	Newcastle	n/a	1	----------L-	1	2	1	▶	0	0	1	2-1 (1x)	27	6
	2nd Oct	Bolton	n/a	1	----------D-	1	1	0	▶	0	0	0	1-1 (1x)	90	5
	16th Oct	Norwich	n/a	These teams have never played each other in the Premiership											
	23rd Oct	C Palace	n/a	These teams have never played each other in the Premiership											
	30th Oct	Chelsea	n/a	1	----------L-	0	2	0	▶	0	0	0	0-2 (1x)	N/A	2
	6th Nov	Southampton	n/a	1	----------L-	0	1	0	▶	0	0	0	1-0 (1x)	N/A	3
	14th Nov	Middlesbro	n/a	1	----------W-	1	0	1	▶	1	0	0	1-0 (1x)	72	6
	20th Nov	Arsenal	n/a	1	----------L-	2	5	0	▶	0	0	0	5-2 (1x)	51	1
	27th Nov	Man Utd	n/a	1	----------L-	1	3	1	▶	0	0	1	1-3 (1x)	6	2
	4th Dec	Portsmouth	n/a	These teams have never played each other in the Premiership											
	11th Dec	Charlton	n/a	1	----------L-	0	1	0	▶	0	0	0	0-1 (1x)	N/A	6
	18th Dec	Birmingham	n/a	1	----------L-	0	1	0	▶	0	0	0	1-0 (1x)	N/A	3
	26th Dec	Liverpool	n/a	1	----------L-	0	6	0	▶	0	0	0	0-6 (1x)	N/A	4

Home fixture

Date	Opposition	03-04 scoreline	Played	Premiership history	Goals for	Goals against	⚽	▶	W	D	L	Most common score (no. times)	Avg time of first goal (mins)	Avg no. of corners	
28th Dec	Man City	n/a	1	----------W-	2	1	1	▶	1	0	0	1-2 (1x)	18	6	
1st Jan	Bolton	n/a	1	----------D-	1	1	1	▶	0	1	0	1-1 (1x)	17	4	
3rd Jan	Newcastle	n/a	1	----------D-	2	2	0	▶	0	0	0	2-2 (1x)	57	2	
15th Jan	Fulham	n/a	1	----------L-	0	3	0	▶	0	0	0	3-0 (1x)	N/A	3	
22nd Jan	Man City	n/a	1	----------L-	1	2	0	▶	0	0	0	1-2 (1x)	62	5	⚽
1st Feb	C Palace	n/a	These teams have never played each other in the Premiership												⚽
5th Feb	Norwich	n/a	These teams have never played each other in the Premiership												
12th Feb	Southampton	n/a	1	----------W-	1	0	1	▶	1	0	0	1-0 (1x)	79		⚽
26th Feb	Chelsea	n/a	1	----------L-	0	2	0	▶	0	0	0	2-0 (1x)	N/A	5	
5th Mar	Birmingham	n/a	1	----------D-	1	1	0	▶	0	0	0	1-1 (1x)	87	11	⚽
19th Mar	Charlton	n/a	1	----------L-	0	1	0	▶	0	0	0	1-0 (1x)	N/A	10	
2nd Apr	Everton	n/a	1	----------L-	1	2	1	▶	0	0	1	1-2 (1x)	18	3	⚽
9th Apr	Aston Villa	n/a	1	----------L-	1	2	0	▶	0	0	0	2-1 (1x)	29	3	
16th Apr	Blackburn	n/a	1	----------L-	0	2	0	▶	0	0	0	0-2 (1x)	N/A	7	⚽
20th Apr	Tottenham	n/a	1	----------L-	1	3	0	▶	0	0	0	3-1 (1x)	73	3	
23rd Apr	Middlesbro	n/a	1	----------L-	0	3	0	▶	0	0	0	3-0 (1x)	N/A	5	
30th Apr	Arsenal	n/a	1	----------L-	1	2	1	▶	0	0	1	1-2 (1x)	3	3	⚽
7th May	Man Utd	n/a	1	----------L-	0	1	0	▶	0	0	0	1-0 (1x)	N/A	1	
14th May	Portsmouth	n/a	These teams have never played each other in the Premiership												⚽

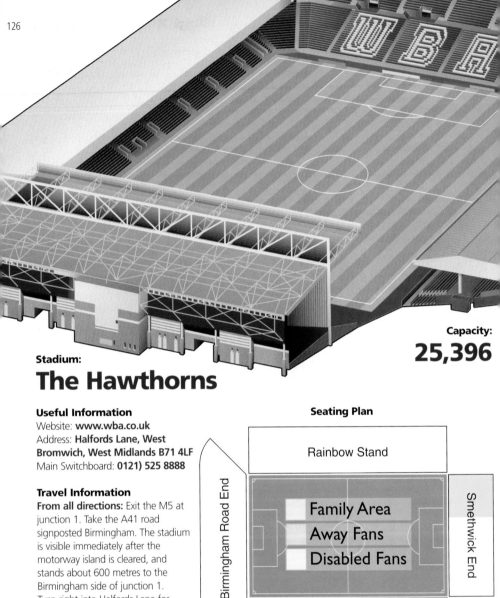

Capacity:
25,396

Stadium:
The Hawthorns

Useful Information
Website: **www.wba.co.uk**
Address: **Halfords Lane, West Bromwich, West Midlands B71 4LF**
Main Switchboard: **0121) 525 8888**

Travel Information
From all directions: Exit the M5 at junction 1. Take the A41 road signposted Birmingham. The stadium is visible immediately after the motorway island is cleared, and stands about 600 metres to the Birmingham side of junction 1. Turn right into Halfords Lane for stadium and car parking.

Seating Plan

Rainbow Stand

Birmingham Road End

Family Area
Away Fans
Disabled Fans

Smethwick End

Halford's Lane (Main) Stand

Area Map

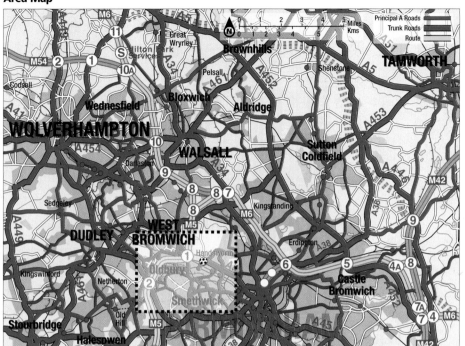

Local Map

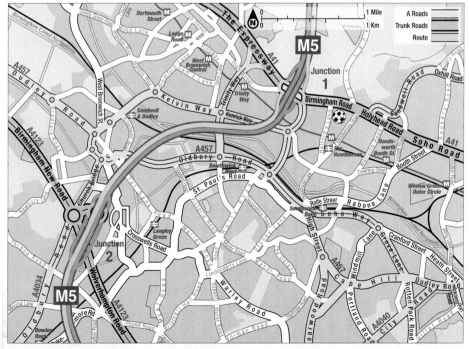

Premiership Fixture Grid 2004-05

	West Brom	Tottenham	Southampton	Portsmouth	Norwich City	Newcastle Utd	Middlesbrough	Manchester Utd	Manchester City	Liverpool	Fulham	Everton	Crystal Palace	Chelsea	Charlton	Bolton	Blackburn	Birmingham	Aston Villa	Arsenal
Arsenal	30/04	13/11	26/02	19/12	28/08	29/12	09/04	24/10	25/09	28/11	11/09	15/08	06/11	20/04	01/01	15/01	19/03	14/05	05/02	
Aston Villa	22/08	30/04	16/04	12/02	18/09	02/04	18/12	22/01	27/11	14/05	02/02	30/10	03/01	26/12	24/01	13/11	02/10	19/03		16/10
Birmingham	05/03	28/08	24/10	14/08	07/05	01/01	11/09	05/02	20/04	06/11	28/12	23/04	26/02	09/04	15/01	25/09	21/11		12/12	04/12
Blackburn	16/04	14/05	21/08	15/01	06/11	11/09	05/02	02/04	13/11	26/02	27/11	05/03	11/12	23/10	27/09	28/12		30/04	01/01	24/08
Bolton	02/10	23/10	25/08	07/05	11/12	26/02	07/11	26/12	05/03	02/04	21/08	04/12	05/02	20/11	16/04		22/01	03/01	23/04	18/09
Charlton	11/12	06/11	26/12	09/04	23/04	05/02	26/02	20/11	23/10	05/03	22/01	05/12	07/05	14/08		16/04	15/01	03/01	02/10	11/09
Chelsea	30/10	15/01	02/04	28/12	05/03	14/05	25/09	16/04	16/10	01/01	13/11	12/02	24/08		27/11	30/04	02/02	21/08	11/09	12/12
Crystal Palace	01/02	28/12	27/11	11/09	14/08	30/04	28/08	18/12	15/01	13/11	01/01	09/04		19/03	14/05	16/04	30/10	25/09	12/02	02/11
Everton	02/04	01/01	05/02	26/09	23/10	28/11	15/01	25/09	11/09	19/03	30/04		21/08	06/11	28/12	14/05	18/12	13/11	26/02	16/04
Fulham	18/09	26/12	03/01	30/08	04/12	06/11	19/03	19/04	14/08	05/02		20/11	04/10	23/04	20/12	09/04	07/05	22/01	23/10	26/02
Liverpool	26/12	14/08	22/01	19/04	03/01	05/03	20/11	09/04	20/09		16/10	11/12	23/04	03/04	01/02	29/08	30/10	12/02	04/12	07/05
Manchester City	22/01	19/03	02/02	20/11	26/02	23/10	06/12	07/11		21/08	16/04	26/12	18/09	05/02	02/04	18/12	23/04	24/08	07/05	03/01
Manchester Utd	27/11	25/09	14/05	30/10	09/04	14/11	01/01		12/02	15/01	13/12	20/04	05/03	15/08	30/04	11/09	28/08	16/10	28/12	01/02
Middlesbrough	14/11	27/11	11/12	01/02	22/01	16/04		02/10	14/05	30/04	25/02	18/09	02/04	03/01	30/10	12/02	05/03	07/05	25/09	22/08
Newcastle Utd	03/01	09/04	19/09	19/03	19/04		14/08	23/04	02/02	18/12	12/02	07/05	20/11	04/12	17/10	31/10	26/12	02/01	28/08	22/01
Norwich City	16/10	12/09	30/04	01/01		25/08	28/12	21/08	01/11	25/09	14/05	02/02	13/11	19/03	12/02	27/11	15/01	02/04	18/12	04/12
Portsmouth	14/05	05/02	13/11		02/10	11/12	23/10	26/02	30/04	25/08	02/04	03/01	26/12	22/01	21/08	15/09	16/04	06/11	05/03	30/10
Southampton	12/02	18/12		23/04	20/11	15/01	19/03	04/12	01/01	28/12	16/10	07/05	28/08	15/09	19/04	09/04	01/02	02/04	30/10	22/11
Tottenham	25/08		05/03	18/10	12/02	26/12	01/02	11/12	07/05	03/01	22/02	19/09	30/10	02/10	02/01	19/03	14/05	04/12	25/09	25/04
West Brom		20/04	06/11	04/12	05/02	25/09	23/04	07/05	28/12	11/09	19/03	01/01	14/08	18/12	09/04	18/09	19/09	23/10	27/11	20/11